Nlp

The Essential Guide to Neurolinguistic Programming

(Fast and Easy Neuro Linguistic Programming Techniques to Change Your Life)

Alberto Larson

Published By **Regina Loviusher**

Alberto Larson

All Rights Reserved

Nlp: The Essential Guide to Neuro-linguistic Programming (Fast and Easy Neuro Linguistic Programming Techniques to Change Your Life)

ISBN 978-1-7771996-9-2

No part of this guidebook shall be reproduced in any form without permission in writing from the publisher except in the case of brief quotations embodied in critical articles or reviews.

Legal & Disclaimer

The information contained in this book is not designed to replace or take the place of any form of medicine or professional medical advice. The information in this book has been provided for educational & entertainment purposes only.

The information contained in this book has been compiled from sources deemed reliable, and it is accurate to the best of the Author's knowledge; however, the Author cannot guarantee its accuracy and validity and cannot be held liable for any errors or omissions. Changes are periodically made to this book. You must consult your doctor or get professional medical advice before using any of the suggested remedies, techniques, or information in this book.

Upon using the information contained in this book, you agree to hold harmless the Author from and against any damages, costs, and expenses, including any legal fees potentially resulting from the application of any of the information provided by this guide. This disclaimer applies to any damages or injury caused by the use and application, whether directly or indirectly, of any advice or information presented, whether for breach of contract, tort, negligence, personal injury, criminal intent, or under any other cause of action.

You agree to accept all risks of using the information presented inside this book. You need to consult a professional medical practitioner in order to ensure you are both able and healthy enough to participate in this program.

Table Of Contents

Chapter 1: Psychological Polarization 1

Chapter 2: Being Polarized Makes you Easy to Control 15

Chapter 3: What are Pattern Interrupts? 30

Chapter 4: How to Use Pattern Interrupts for Influence 49

Chapter 5: The Benjamin Franklin Effect 63

Chapter 6: Charisma and Love Bombing 79

Chapter 7: Combining Charisma with the Love Bomb Technique........................... 95

Chapter 8: Inspire Fear, then Relief...... 113

Chapter 9: Four Frames you Can Manipulate 128

Chapter 10: Suggestibility Testing 143

Chapter 11: Your Life Can Look Different 151

Chapter 12: What Is NLP used for? 162

Chapter 13: Installed Predetermination 170

Chapter 14: Program Update 181

Chapter 1: Psychological Polarization

What is Psychological Polarization?

What makes companies of rational humans grow to be a mob? Why is it that humans adopt the ideals and behavior of others whilst they come together in a fixed? Why do human beings's opinions grow to be extra immoderate when they rally with others of the identical mentality? In order to understand these questions, we need to check the concept of mental polarization.

You have probable heard the time period "fanning the flames" however possibly you haven't given it lots concept because it pertains to human beings's attitudes and psychologies. This is a herbal omission but the fact of the hassle is that it is a pretty apt analogy for what takes place to human beings once they undergo intellectual polarization.

Psychological polarization takes area even as one unearths that their views or evaluations are in stark competition to a person else's. Polarization will become more excessive when an opposing opinion or notion becomes more vocal or apparent.

Two people sitting in a room collectively can get to speaking about the towns wherein they stay — an innocent verbal exchange that may grow to be polarizing when they start talking approximately why they assume their cities are better than others. Now rational adults who've been accomplishing fine small speak in the meantime are cut up into discord with one retaining firmly to one opinion on the equal time because the alternative holds firmly to an opposing opinion.

That is mental polarization and it has a effective impact at the manner we count on, on our attitudes and the process by manner of which we make alternatives. So wherein does the "fanning the flames" analogy comes into play in phrases of intellectual polarization? Take the aforementioned example of the two adults sitting together and discussing the cities wherein they stay. Now don't forget that there are 2 more people in that equal room accomplishing that equal verbal exchange. The threat that the ones new human beings will take aspects within the argument is all however high-quality.

Now you have got were given have been given 4 humans in a room at odds with each different over a effective assignment count range. In this setting, a few detail uncommon begins offevolved offevolved to take place. The extra humans you add to this debate, the wider the argumentative hole the various businesses grows and the polarization turns into greater intense. This is what's referred to as organisation polarization: the phenomenon thru which polarization turns into greater excessive as more people engage in the situation. That little flame that grow to be the communication approximately towns receives fanned with virtually every person you upload to it.

Group polarization can sweep towards the opportunity excessive too. When you get a set of like-minded humans collectively, their beliefs typically become being more affirmed and radical than within the occasion that they've been left to their very own devices. There are some one-of-a-kind reasons for this phenomenon. One of them is simple enough to recognize: at the same time as you offer humans a discussion board to talk to one another approximately a given state of affairs, they may be capable of percentage their reviews and make a case for what it's far they consider in. This is referred to as persuasion and some human beings are amazing at it. Not anybody have to be correct at persuasion regardless of the reality that. There are some folks which can be clearly more inclined and open to having their minds changed or adopting a greater enthusiastic view on a few element than others.

When you get a difficult and fast of humans collectively and get them to speak about one element or each different, someone is high-quality to be persuaded one way or the alternative so that is one manner that institution polarization can stand up.

Another way you could apprehend polarization is as peer strain, but within the psychology worldwide it's miles known as 'assessment'. In a set putting, a few human beings are tremendous to sense compelled to yield to the opinion of the bulk and compromise their very personal beliefs for ones which might be more in step with the herd. People start evaluating themselves and what they assume with others and their very own perspectives are skewed through the collective lens of the organisation.

Lastly, institution polarization can rise up even as an individual evaluates their ideals in evaluation to what the institution she or he is in ought to be about. In distinctive words, someone may not always be in choice of capital punishment but revel in that their company need to in the end suggest for it. This is a mild tweaking of someone's critiques for what they understand the extra real of the organization ought to be.

Group polarization may be visible in motion pretty thousands every day. All one might want to do is have a take a look at the observation segment of any random YouTube video to appearance how people align themselves to at the least one facet of an issue or opinion over every specific. Parents who've attended a PTA assembly have probable seen institution polarization in motion as properly. Maybe the locale of the sixth grade location journey end up placed to a vote and you observed one group choose the zoo even as some different enterprise voted for the artwork museum.

If you are an person you have got were given probable gotten right into a debate about religion or politics in some unspecified time in the future too. Religion and politics are some of the rifest forums for dissent and polarization because of ego identity. Ego identity is what offers the person a feel of self inside the face of changing instances. Ego identification allows someone to have a notion of themselves even in mild of the perceptions that different people have of them. Put it this manner: there can be the you that exists for your mom's mind, there is the you that exists to your pal's mind, there's the you that exists for your co-worker's thoughts and it is going on and on with each unmarried individual you apprehend or sincerely meet. Then there may be the you that exists for your private thoughts and this model of you is primarily based upon largely to your ego identity.

Many people assist develop an ego identification, a buoying, non-wavering version of themselves that they are able to hang to even if everything else in their lifestyles can be strong into doubt, thru faith or politics or every. Religion and politics have a propensity to be made into intellectual secure havens that the individual can understand themselves with. People recollect in those tenants so rigidly because of the reality to desert them or modify them is probably tantamount to leaving in the back of or changing themselves – or as a minimum, who they have believed themselves to be for max in their lives. It is lots simpler to take a look at a route down its remaining avenue than to form a current day ego identification for one's self it certainly is why humans draw near so fervently to their political opinions and non secular ideals and moreover why they are such ripe fields for polarization.

Divide and Conquer

The idea of intellectual polarization is a key precept to understand while thinking about the darker side of psychology. Many mental manipulators use this principle to their advantage. Think approximately it - in case you understand that human beings's reviews (even deeply held opinions) are vulnerable to change in a fixed context, and that people will most in all likelihood be conditioned to the frequently taking vicinity psychology of the group, then you may 'fan the flames' and create conditions in which humans act predictably.

Clever intellectual manipulators construct faux dichotomies, information complete well that human beings will probably gravitate to one thing or the alternative. Let's go returned to take a look at the quote on the start of the financial disaster: "Religion is regarded through manner of the common people as actual, thru the clever as fake, and with the resource of way of the rulers as beneficial." What does this mean precisely? It approach that it does no longer depend what is real or fake; what topics is that you may expect how humans will react, and use that on your advantage.

Does your loyalty to your sports activities activities sports activities organization make you higher than your neighbor? Is your religion extra real and righteous than unique human beings's? Does your manual for the Democratic or Republican celebration make you smarter than different people that you realise? When you select out out with businesses, your ego identification will become worried, and also you become reactive in place of logical. If you're aware of how this recreation works, it will move an extended manner in information dark psychology and manipulation.

Problem, Reaction Solution The Hegelian Dialectic

The Hegelian Dialectic is a contrived technique of solving a conflict or polarization. An opinion, concept, notion or thesis is provided with the purpose to without a doubt have a counter opinion, idea, perception or thesis. The 2 opposing thesis and antithesis are then resolved within the Hegelian Dialectic with a synthesis or a melding of each the authentic thesis and antithesis.

In different terms, gift a trouble to which you apprehend an character or institution will take a stance in competition to and provide a compromise or a manner to the struggle. This technique may be seen as a in no way-completing way of warfare selection because of the reality with every synthesis or answer amongst opposing mind, you're truely handiest growing every different thesis for someone to rally in competition to.

Karl Marx primarily based a good deal of his political philosophy inside the Hegelian Dialectic but he purported that there has been sincerely a very final vacation spot that would spawn no in addition conflicts. For him the very last holiday spot, the answer to all conflicts and polarization modified into the belief of the utopian communist society. It is arguable whether or not or no longer or now not Marx absolutely believed that there can be a few form of forestall component to any new release of the Hegelian Dialectic or if he genuinely purported this principle to govern the hundreds towards his very own beliefs but one trouble is sure: the Hegelian Dialectic is a powerful tool for dark manipulation.

The way the darkish manipulator effectively makes use of the Hegelian Dialectic to his or her advantage is by way of having a synthesis or solution in thoughts in advance than ever providing a hassle to rally in opposition to.

For instance, allow's say you recognize that you need pizza for dinner but your buddy needs a burger. You tell your pal that you could get ground pork, tomatoes, onions or even cheese on a pizza however you can't get pepperoni and a doughy crust on a burger. You provide pizza as a truthful compromise amongst you're his choice to have a burger and your preference to have a pizza but in the end, you one manner or the alternative managed to get one hundred% of what you want whilst your pal is left with a few compromised model of what he or she desired.

A darker instance; say a person dreams the opportunity to scouse borrow subjects from people's homes with minimum chance of being stuck. Someone have to use the Hegelian Dialectic to spark war between residents and the police to incite a riot, consequently making it less complex for the character to loot at will without a effects. This individual need to spread the rumor that the police were brutalizing citizens indiscriminately thereby creating a hassle for the citizenry.

Chapter 2: Being Polarized Makes you Easy to Control

You can be asking your self what polarization and the Hegelian Dialectic must do with each one-of-a-type. The technique to that is the whole lot. When someone is privy to a way to push your buttons – what your ego identification is based totally mostly on – they may be capable of purpose you to sense or react in a predictable manner.

Telling a person already distrustful of police that they really beat up an innocent citizen for no motive is an easy manner to get that individual riled up. So how is that useful for manipulation?

When human beings input a polarized emotional country they normally have a propensity to behave in techniques that they generally might not. Going decrease again to the idea of business organisation polarization, it's miles been confirmed time and time over again that people's beliefs and willingness to make excessive choices are ramped up notably at the same time as they're in a hard and fast of like-minded individuals.

If you may are anticipating the manner someone may furthermore react when provided with certain incensing stimuli, you'll be able to are expecting the manner a hard and fast of similar humans will react. When you can expect the manner an entire organisation will react, you have upped your electricity of manipulation from swaying one person to swaying a whole institution.

This swaying of a tough and rapid exponentially grows your manipulation energy as nicely because humans will act greater rashly in a fixed than they might on their very own consequently developing a greater powerful sweep inside the course which you, the manipulator favors.

How Polarized are you?

It's time to check your self. Being polarized technique that you could be effects manipulated by means of way of others. You in no manner want to be the sheep; you usually need to be the shepherd, on top of things of your very private feelings. To see how polarized you might be, attempt asking yourself some questions:

How critically do you are taking your ideals?

Are you unwilling to alternate your opinion on any given subject matter based totally mostly on precept on my own?

Do you've got an open thoughts approximately different people's reviews?

Has every person for your lifestyles actually persuaded you to exchange your thoughts about a certain topic?

Have you ever gotten indignant whilst overhearing a communication in which a person is voicing an opinion opposite to yours?

Do you may be predisposed to stay calm eventually of debates or arguments?

Do you enjoy a deep dislike for terrific political or religious businesses?

Do you'll be predisposed to lose your cool while confronted with hostility or conflict of any kind?

If you replied sure to any of these questions then you may advantage from wearing activities that might help train you to emerge as extra emotionally and mentally unbiased. An incensed united states of america of the usa is a breeding ground for irrational idea and movement. And irrational perception and motion will serve you up on a silver platter to the whims of a cunning manipulator. In order to train yourself to be more mentally and emotionally independent, try a few or all the following:

Keep your sentences short and succinct on the equal time as arguing with a person.

Anticipate counterarguments in your private elements so you are organized for the worst that a person ought to mention.

Rehearse your response to conditions you enjoy you might be the most distressed in.

Practice retaining a straight away, non-telling look for your face.

Find a beneficial distraction whilst you begin to sense incensed like locating a superb shape or colour in the right away vicinity or counting the huge form of high-quality devices which you see around you.

Cardio workout is a wonderful manner to alleviate stress so you are better geared up to stay independent in the face of polarizing conditions.

Avoid conditions which may be likely to have a polarizing effect on you and intoxicating yourself in order that you will be consequences polarized.

It can take some exercising, however depolarizing your self and gaining knowledge of to control your feelings will make you very tough to manipulate, at the same time as on the same time permitting you to appearance and anticipate how others can be manipulated.

The Four Stages of Hypnosis

Why you Should Master the Four Stages of Hypnosis

Let's talk a few unique foundational precept of darkish psychology and manipulation: hypnosis. Hypnosis is certainly pretty easy to apprehend in case you understard the way it works. Of direction, it takes exercising to grasp hypnotising others; however, absolutely data the manner it really works can be very useful in being able to have a examine dark psychology and manipulation in workout.

Hypnosis has a bent to be misunderstood as a parlor trick that requires a person to be asleep or in a nearly asleep country so you can turn out to be hypnotized. Then, whilst they're under the spell of hypnosis, they will be made to cluck like a fowl or bark like a dog or repeat any amount of embarrassing terms for a cheap chuckle. The fact is that hypnosis occurs each day due to the reality all hypnosis approach is that someone has entered into an altered nation, or a trance usa.

We enter trance states every day. All it takes to go into a trance kingdom is to hitch your interest on one aspect so cautiously that some or all your peripheral attention can be close out. Most humans, for example, input a hypnotic country every day at paintings or zoning out on the equal time as on the subway.

Hypnosis may be a high-quality tool for getting humans to compromise their essential faculties and it ties into what we were talking approximately to this point in terms of polarization and eliciting a favored reaction from someone. We talked about how you may obtain this thru the Hegelian Dialectic, but it's also important to apprehend the 4 degrees of hypnosis because it will significantly gain you in terms of the strategies that we can delve into in some time on this e book.

Stage 1: Absorb Attention

The first step into changing someone's conscious state (hypnosis) is grabbing preserve in their full hobby. Believe it or now not, there are verbal and non-verbal styles of this primary degree of hypnosis. Take, for instance, the aforementioned state of affairs wherein a person may be so zoned in at artwork that the entirety round them type of in reality fades away.

This is a excessive example of the manner that our intellectual states are changed even as we're in reality carefully focused on something and of non-verbal hypnosis.

Of route, gaining a person's entire and whole hobby can be a bit less complicated in case you are the use of phrases. People have a tendency to preserve more without a doubt to a person's terms at the same time as they're describing photos or telling a tale. It is lots like how some human beings pick out visible mastering over textual getting to know. The human mind can observe along higher on the same time as photos and highbrow images are involved, because of the fact their seen enjoy is engaged.

You can exercising this number one level of hobby absorption in regular speech. Go out with a pal or coworker and be aware how masses extra they be aware of you on the same time as you say you have got have been given a story for them. Tell them a story, both actual or made up, and make sure to encompass hundreds of records. Paint the picture with your phrases, use quite some adjectives to offer an cause of the scene. The greater senses you may interact, the higher. Give their mind and creativeness a few component to engage with.

When you have them wrapped up for your tale, you have successfully absorbed their interest so that it will lead you into the second degree of hypnosis:

Stage 2: Bypass the Critical Faculty

The conscious mind is a as a substitute constrained entity. It takes in the information this is thrown at you each day and it methods it rationally. The unconscious thoughts rather is a lot greater whimsical. It does no longer get bogged down with subjects of reality. Consider, for example, that your unconscious thoughts is lively whilst you dream. You may additionally moreover have in no way visible a crimson, flying turtle in real lifestyles but your subconscious mind is loose to hold in mind things like simply actual and possible.

The conscious mind gives with what is feasible, and in hypnosis, that is what's known as the crucial college. Think of the crucial school as a mum or dad at the gate to the unconscious thoughts. The vital college is what signs your mind to matters that aren't feasible, unreasonable and not going. If you are trying to hypnotise a person, the essential university is the enemy of hypnosis. The factor of hypnosis is transferring a person's thoughts from a very aware country to an subconscious or as a minimum an altered nation, and the essential faculties make it no longer feasible for this transfer to arise so it have to be bypassed.

Bypassing the important colleges can be completed via first soaking up the whole attention of someone as we honestly mentioned and with the useful resource of the usage of a few simple techniques which incorporates preserving purpose eye-contact with the trouble and speakme a touch slower and decrease than you commonly do.

Speaking in a hypnotic tone can bypass an prolonged way in inciting a trance us of a and bypassing the essential college. If you're hypnotising someone, you want to observe out for symptoms and symptoms that your state of affairs is in a trance country. Most importantly, do no longer deliver any hypnotic guidelines till you're sure you are past the crucial university and your difficulty is in a trance nation - otherwise, your concept can be rejected via the crucial college.

Step 3: Activate an Unconscious Response

Activating an subconscious reaction does now not ought to be as immoderate as getting a person to cluck like a fowl. It can be as diffused as evoking amusing or making a person clap their hands to their mouth in surprise. An unconscious response is any movement completed that someone isn't aware of or is best aware about after the movement has been made. In distinctive words, it's miles a reaction that has now not been regulated by means of way of the usage of the aware mind.

Eliciting an unconscious response may be very clean even as someone has entered a hypnotic country. Look for a dilation of the scholars, a change in breathing price or a flushing of the pores and pores and skin. These are all signs and symptoms and signs and symptoms and signs and symptoms that your trouble has let their vital university defend down and had been ushered proper into a hypnotic nation.

Once you take a look at this, try eliciting an unconscious reaction; likely describe in shiny element a tasty steak dinner truly so their stomachs growl in starvation or a swarm of bugs overtaking someone's frame in order that their skin crawls with goosebumps.

Stage four: Lead to Your Desired Outcome

This is the factor in which you, the hypnotist, can lead the challenge in the course of a desired very last results via hypnotic idea or associated metaphors. This level of hypnotism is all approximately talking right now to the unconscious thoughts and taking gain of the altered united states of america to both assist the character, or to manual them to a cease, final consequences or preference that is favorable for you.

Chapter 3: What are Pattern Interrupts?

The concept of pattern interrupts is virtually very simple. Consider each word in my view: the number one word within the phrase being "pattern." A pattern can be something you do mindlessly or habitually. Getting up within the morning, brushing your tooth and taking a shower is probable some thing you do each day which you don't even in reality think about. This is an example of a pattern. A pattern also may be known as a regular. Getting in your automobile and using to paintings may be considered a recurring.

Now bear in mind the second one word in the phrase: "interrupt." An interrupt in this context is something that breaks your everyday exercises or styles. Interrupts are conscious efforts to change the manner you do things, the way you observed or the way you act.

The main distinction between the two terms – the two requirements of "sample" and "interrupt" – is that one includes an unconscious or passive u . S . A . Of thoughts and the possibility involves a very aware and active u.S. Of the usa of mind.

Pattern interrupts are regularly used in behavioral psychology and NLP to assist people smash dangerous behavior and bodily video games of their lives. Routines frequently supply us a revel in of strength and purpose however they may be destructive at the identical time as we get so used to them that we transfer off our brains even as doing them, thereby turning into vulnerable to hypnotic concept and manipulation.

The common human has approximately 50,000 mind consistent with day however the majority of those are repeat mind. Pattern interrupts are very powerful techniques to result in new mind which permits the mind growth its functionality to assume severely. It is the distinction amongst letting your mind atrophy and exercising it.

To get once more to fundamentals, take into account sample interrupts a manner to alter yours or a person else's highbrow united states of america from a aware to an unconscious mode. This is precisely why sample interrupts can be used for hypnosis and NLP.

In precise, sample interrupts may be very useful for instant hypnotic induction or getting a person right into a hypnotic america of america right away. This is due to the truth there may be a slight disconnect in someone's thoughts at the same time as a sample interrupt is used on them. The transfer from passive to active brain function isn't seamless. There is a lapse in which the subconscious and aware thoughts meld for a short time and it is in this time that someone enters a hypnotic u.S. And is at risk of idea.

Consider it a country of bewilderment that someone enters for a fast time while one in each in their patterns or concept techniques is all of sudden interrupted. As a consider of truth, confusion strategies are very not unusual and powerful techniques of rapid hypnotic induction.

Remember the instance of polarization we went over inside the first bankruptcy? Pattern interrupts and confusion are corresponding to polarization within the experience that each are used to get someone right into a body of thoughts in which their reactions may be anticipated and manipulated.

Getting a person riled up about a effective assignment is much like setting someone proper into a stressed u . S . A . In which their recurring has been broken. It is in this nation that a professional hypnotist can implant unconscious belief and consequently predict a positive final results.

Pattern interrupt techniques have come to be very famous in hypnosis and manipulation because of the truth they're pretty easy to carry out and they will be performed in definitely any placing and from time to time with out the individual even know-how it. It happens in an proper now and garners the desired outcomes in an at once that is why it has turn out to be such an oft used tool to hypnotize and control humans.

The most well-known technique of sample interrupt hypnotic induction is the handshake technique. In this approach, the hypnotist will pass in for the very mundane act of shaking someone's hand and at the final 2d earlier than the palms clearly contact, one person disengages from the handshake and grabs the opposite individual via way of the wrist.

This sudden jolt and damage in a normal pattern is a microcosm example of the macro examples that have been touched on in the starting of this monetary catastrophe. Getting up and getting organized for art work is a regular that might take hours and shaking a person's hand first-rate takes some seconds, but they may be each styles and they might both be broken and at the identical time as they're, the thoughts enters an altered us of a.

This altered u.S. Is the aim of sample interrupts and why they will be this form of powerful device for inducing hypnotic trances.

How to Induce Hypnosis With a Pattern Interrupt

Going decrease again once more to a idea stated inside the previous bankruptcy, hobby absorbing is similar to sample interrupts for inducing hypnosis. Pattern interrupts are surely another method of grabbing someone's full hobby and it is able to be argued that hypnosis isn't always whatever however getting someone to be clearly gift in the moment.

The aim of the hypnotist isn't to knock a person out or make a person subconscious. It is to intensify their sense of reputation through whole interest absorption. The motive that sample interrupts are so useful for commanding the whole lot of an individual's interest (consequently leaving them susceptible to hypnotic belief) is that after someone's educate of idea is right away broken, the thoughts is frantically searching out a logical purpose for the interrupt.

It may be as clean as interrupting someone mid-sentence. Let's say you get your buddy telling you a tale approximately a run-in that that they had at a grocery maintain or a battle of words that they had with someone that bumped into them on the street. Try interrupting them in the middle of the story with a completely unrelated phrase "I actually have typically puzzled what makes the moon so silvery."

Your pal emerge as virtually engaged in his or her story and they will have even been in vehicle-pilot if it changed proper right into a tale they've got knowledgeable a couple of times earlier than. When you interrupted them collectively together with your statement about the moon, you broke their notion sample and now their interest is 100% on you and why you interrupted them and what the shade of the moon has to do with their story.

This leaves them in a susceptible country of hypnotic perception because of the fact they are now putting in your every phrase in a determined attempt to get solutions. And in with a purpose to those answers come from? You, of course. It is in this very moment that hypnotists can implant their hypnotic suggestion which can do not have some issue to do with what the person end up talking or thinking about.

This works due to the truth at the equal time because the thoughts is engaged in a sample, it is definitely engaged in carrying out the pattern to its logical give up. When the pattern is skillfully damaged the thoughts immediately recoils and both is seeking out a new pattern or attempting to find to satisfy the antique sample.

Imagine a person on foot through a winding hall and recollect that you can flip the lights out within the hall and make it absolutely dark. When you turn the lighting out the character can't see a factor and has no dependable way to navigate this winding hall. They are searching to expose the lights again on and be on their manner yet again. Then, you switch the lighting fixtures once more on and they might see.

The susceptible kingdom of whilst the character is within the dark and is trying to get the lighting fixtures on yet again is much like what the brain reports while its idea sample has been interrupted. It is looking to show the lights once more on just so it is able to get again at the right song with the pattern.

Now permit's say you don't flip the lighting on until you've got noticed that the person traversing this hall has absolutely grew to turn out to be themselves spherical in a frantic search for a mild transfer. They do now not take a look at that they may be now going via the opportunity path that they have been taking walks in and start strolling in the incorrect course.

This is largely the idea of implanting a hypnotic concept when you have effectively broken the highbrow sample of an person. You get their minds entering into a very wonderful path than it became earlier than, similar to you stressed the person inside the corridor with darkness to the point that they begin on foot the wrong way. The direction the man or woman become taking walks emerge as the pattern and the darkness in this example is consultant of the sample interrupt.

This is how a professional hypnotist can manipulate the way a person speaks after they had been inducted with a sample interrupt.

Hypnotists use pattern interruption to get the thoughts stepping into a certain route. Let's say as an instance your partner asks you "Can you hand me the frying pan?" and also you solution "Yes" however don't hand it to them. You have sincerely answered their question with a yes and damaged the path that their mind turn out to be heading in due to the fact now they'll be thinking about the uncommon reaction to a mundane query.

You have your partner's undivided interest now and suppose you preserve through pronouncing "Settle. You don't ought to fry some issue for what we are eating tonight."

The first phrase in that phrase, "settle" end up truly a hypnotic command just like the cliché "sleep" or "relax" and it set the tone for the rest of the hypnotic idea. This is simply considered one of hundreds of methods that a hypnotist can bring about a hypnotic kingdom through pattern interrupts.

Examples of Pattern Interrupts in Real Life

The brilliant factor approximately pattern interrupts is that they may be used any day, any time and in otherwise ordinary settings. You don't want to have your personal administrative center that allows you to implant a hypnotic belief in a person's thoughts using pattern interrupts.

Not only can sample interrupts be deployed definitely everywhere and in any scenario however they can be used for mental manipulation. You have in all likelihood been the state of affairs or at least visible a psychological manipulation in motion the use of pattern interrupts. They arise all the time without absolutely everyone records it.

There is a completely easy way to manipulate humans that pretty masses each person can do but even this base tactic is an example of a success psychological manipulation thru pattern interruption. Picture if you may, a state of affairs wherein your accomplice is deep in concept approximately what to make for dinner. You need hen however you have not any idea what your partner is imagining making. Suddenly showing her a chit within the paper or a particularly attractive video online for hen recipe can damage their cognizance on something sort of meals they were considering cooking and gets a present day teach of notion taking place chicken. You have effectively used a pattern interrupt to control the state of affairs and heightened your chances of getting fowl for dinner.

Another method of sample interrupt is some issue called overload. The idea behind overload is to manipulate someone's notion method or feelings through pushing them past a threshold of tolerance. The way you could push someone past this threshold is with the beneficial resource of feeding them photographs or vibrant rationalization of something and going way over the top with it. Once the imagery becomes an excessive amount of the person can not complete some thing sample they were on.

For instance, allow's say you've got got a pal who doesn't like broccoli. Imagine you describe to this specific friend a dinner you had that featured broccoli and also you defined in copious detail the odor, texture, taste and the feel of the broccoli on your mouth as your tooth shredded via the thick greenery and the roughage of the vegetable. Your buddy will with the useful resource of trying to find to block the imagery however as soon as it gets to be an excessive amount of for them, they'll be driven past their threshold of tolerance and be now not able to push aside this new direction that their mind are taking. Imagine that you were so descriptive of the broccoli that your pal has out of location their appetite or possibly grow to be queasy. This is but every different instance of intellectual manipulation thru pattern interruption.

Another quite simple technique for mental manipulation through sample interrupt is confusion. Confusion is a tactic that is typically used in hypnotherapy as it has a way of disarming an individual. It is used to help people overcome irrational fears, or to permit them to modify topics approximately their individual like becoming more assertive or greater vocal.

Confusion may be used to get the person's thoughts off the tension, anger, fear or a few issue emotion they've got associated with a first-rate concept. Fear of flying is commonly referred to in hypnotherapist places of work and one tactic this is normally used to help customers get over their fears is through getting them to think carefully about the act of flying, what it is about flying that makes them frightened or even having the patient envision in their thoughts the worst viable state of affairs they are capable of be given as true with with regard to flying. Maybe a fiery aircraft crash. When they begin to envision this stuff their thoughts receives taking place a sample of worry and tension as they don't forget their worst nightmares coming real.

The hypnotist will then interrupt their idea technique with a totally complicated string of terms or terms like, "If someone answers a question with a query wouldn't the following question be a option to the preliminary query or could probable the question be a question unto itself and therefore need to reply to the question?" This complicated diction will completely damage the distressing mind of plane crashes in the purchaser's thoughts and replace t with a dilemma this is mild and as a minimum, not lifestyles-endangering.

This flora a seed in the purchaser's thoughts and while achieved correctly, realigns the association that the purchaser makes when they think about flying. Instead of fear and anxiety, the concept of flying is now associated with a feel of ease that came from the sample interrupt of the difficult question that broke the sample of worried mind.

Not nice is the patron disarmed and a number of the edge of the concept of flying has been taken away, however a very good hypnotist could have virtually modified what the customer friends with flying from fear to ease.

Hypnotherapists can also use the overload tactic of sample interrupt for the benefit in their customers. For example, weight loss is some other common problem that patients come to hypnotherapists with. The therapist will then use image or sensory overload to show the patron off of a exquisite fatty meals that they have a tough time resisting. They can use an abundance of photos associated with potato chips, as an example, to push the patron past their threshold of tolerance surely in order that they companion potato chips with an unsightly experience and consequently come to be an increasing number of averse to them.

Chapter 4: How to Use Pattern Interrupts for Influence

Pattern interrupts are effective equipment for impact as well because of the reality they may be capable of ship a person's thoughts right into a malleable us of a that you can use to your advantage or for the benefit of the person. For instance, allow's say which you need to get a dog however your spouse or roommate is terrified of dogs and don't want to have one within the residence. Try the following approach that's called the Spin Out approach of sample interruption.

In this method you may:

Engage the individual in verbal exchange approximately their worry of puppies

Ask them what they may be frightened of specially

When they answer, ask them why they may be afraid of that specific element

When they solution, respond with a question approximately what it is that makes them afraid of that first-rate difficulty

When they solution, ask them how they realise that particular hassle is scary

You can keep on and on like this indefinitely. The conversation would possibly pass a few element like this:

You: "What is it about puppies that scares you?"

Them: "I'm afraid they'll chew"

You: "Why are you afraid they will chew?"

Them: "Because it has befell to me."

You: "Why are you scared of being bitten?"

Them: "Because it hurts"

You: "How do you comprehend it harm?"

Them: "Because I felt it."

You: "How do you apprehend you felt it?"

Them: "Because it took place to me."

You: "And how do that biting is frightening?"

By trivializing the good judgment via which a person friends a pleasant fear or emotion you strain the man or woman to impeach the validity of the affiliation. This is called the spin out technique of pattern interrupt as it sends the man or woman's manner of considering a positive affiliation right into a spin. The character will then come to a attention regarding their worry of dogs or abandon their line of reasoning altogether as you've got set them on a brand new pattern through the spin out interrupt.

Everything we've were given were given mentioned in this monetary wreck can be used to get a person proper right into a hypnotic trance. The pattern interrupt technique for inducing trance is an easy manner to obtain a moderate hypnotic united states of america however even those mild states can be a fertile vicinity for hypnotic idea.

Make no mistake approximately it: getting a person off in their initial train of notion and onto some different is a shape of hypnosis and highbrow manipulation. It might also furthermore appear easy but much like an device, it is easy to choose out out up but very hard to apprehend.

Once you have got have been given practiced and become adept at using the pattern interrupt technique for inducing hypnotic trances, you could want to apprehend what to do as quickly as you've got got someone in a trance, that is what we are able to be going over within the following chapters.

Dark NLP Technique 2: Subliminal Messages & Embedded Commands

In the previous couple of chapters, we have got lengthy past over the ideas of coercion thru sample interrupts and inducing a hypnotic or as a minimum and impressionable country. But there can be any other powerful approach of coaxing a person to do high high-quality subjects which has to do with implanting ideas in their minds covertly. These processes are called subliminal messaging and supraliminal messaging.

Unlike the techniques we have mentioned in advance, the ones do not require hypnotizing or in any other case mentally conditioning the priority. Instead, those techniques can be deployed at any time and artwork on the glaringly taking area aware and subconscious levels of our minds. In one of a kind phrases, the sphere is already fertile - you simply need to plant the seeds.

To start with, permit's communicate about subliminal messages and what they're exactly. A subliminal message is any stimuli – it is able to be an image, a phrase or possibly a faint perfume – which is probably registered by way of manner of the mind on an unconscious diploma. They are messages which might be communicated underneath the brink of popularity. You can bear in mind them as indicators or guidelines that barely make it through to you thoughts like Indiana Jones slightly rolling under a huge stone door because it closes close.

Going decrease again to the second one financial ruin wherein we cited the 4 tiers of hypnosis and bypassing the critical university of the aware mind, subliminal messaging moreover has to do with tapping into the unconscious mind and slipping with the aid of using the aware and critical schools of the mind. Again, that is effective for manipulation and NLP due to the fact the subconscious thoughts is greater open to fantastical and otherwise contrary recommendations. It isn't slowed down with the resource of fact or what the conscious thoughts also can comprehend to be proper.

So subliminal messaging is meant to talk to the unconscious thoughts and bypass the essential school of the aware mind. It is kind of a cat burglar sneaking beyond a completely modern day protection device with armed sentinels, stress touchy floors and motion detecting lasers.

You can be statistics now that subliminal messaging is only a success at the same time because the character is a hundred% unaware that they've been communicated to. It is thankless paintings but if you have efficaciously implanted a person with a subliminal message, they may never recognize it. On the flipside, if you have ever been subliminally manipulated you're in all likelihood ignorant of it to this modern.

The subconscious thoughts is lots more susceptible to proposal than the aware thoughts, that is why that is a precious approach to examine. Like hypnosis, the hassle may be more likely to carry out a desired final consequences however not like hypnosis, subliminal messaging requires nearly no priming.

Supraliminal Messaging

With supraliminal messaging, the equal very last consequences is completed however through special way. Supraliminal messaging entails passively appealing the conscious mind to coerce an unconscious response. It impacts subconsciously honestly similar to subliminal messaging however it does no longer bypass the aware thoughts. In supraliminal messaging, the concern is exposed to a stimulus that it is able to be aware about (even though it works exceptional whilst the stimulus operates on the fringes of aware interest), however they may be unaware that this stimulus is affecting them subconsciously and prodding them in the route of a positive outcome or motion.

Supraliminal messaging hinges on the idea that the whole lot in our hobby is associated with some thing else. This is known as the semantic network. The semantic community is the highbrow feature with the beneficial useful resource of that you take into account subjects or revel in high quality emotions at the same time as supplied with a high best stimulus or node. The nodes reply to the stimulus and convey up the semantic network which calls to the leading fringe of your thoughts unique memories, pictures or emotions that stem from the originating node.

You probably use the semantic network every day. For instance, are you the type of person who thinks of the ocean whenever you pay interest the caw of a seagull? Or do you ever get thirsty whilst you pay attention the pop of a newly opened soda can? These are examples of the semantic community at play: any stimulus that triggers certain mind, recollections, pics, mind or emotions.

The semantic community additionally may be invoked to elicit superb actions. This is wherein supraliminal messaging comes into play. You can probable now see what it's miles that separates subliminal and supraliminal messaging: you want the person to consciously check in certain stimulus to elicit an motion in preference to hiding the stimulus under the blanket of the unconscious.

Sublimiral/Supraliminal Messaging at Work

Subliminal messaging has due to the truth that been vilified ever as it got here into public view in the 1950's as it end up purportedly utilized in advertising and marketing. Cola agencies have been accused of flashing phrases a millionth of a 2d of their commercials that allows you to get the purchaser to crave their product no matter the reality that they didn't realize why.

A proper instance of subliminal messaging is on the identical time as a recording artist secretly places a message onto considered considered one of their records. Some had been accused of hiding a spoken message to the listener at frequencies that the conscious thoughts can't find out however even though affect the listener on a subconscious degree.

On your way to art work each day, you may be passing a billboard that modified into mainly designed to have a subliminal effect. These can consist of snap shots hidden internal a larger photograph or a configuration of features within the large photograph that naked a diffused resemblance to a few element else.

Supraliminal messaging can be deployed in everyday existence as properly. If your pal wishes you to go together with them for a walk via the forest, they might spray some pine scented air freshener of their home in advance than you get there to prompt the nodes of your semantic community and incline you towards going with them on a hike through the woods.

The subsequent time you have were given had been given motive to play rock, paper, scissors to settle a dispute, try this trick: earlier than the sport begins, consider a phrase that consists of the phrase "hard." Then say the word right in advance than your duel. When the individual hears the word that contains the word "hard" in it, they will be greater inclined to area down rock seeing that you've were given brought on a node concerning rocks in their minds. Then you can placed down paper and win the dispute.

Likewise, when you have it in mind to throw down rock yourself, try saying "Oh man, I gotta keep sharp for this one" proper earlier than you rectangular off. Your opponent will in all likelihood throw down scissors because of their association of the adjective "sharp" to scissors.

It is a recognized truth that fast meals consuming places use certain colors on their signs and symptoms and houses to awaken starvation. The shades are commonly pink, brown and yellow and that they play on our institutions of these hues to flawlessly cooked pork and appealing condiments that generally accompany burgers.

Chapter 5: The Benjamin Franklin Effect

The Benjamin Franklin impact comes from an incident the diverse founding father and a political opponent. Benjamin Franklin requested this opponent – someone which became no fan of Franklin – to lend him a e-book; a modest need so the opponent became obliged to consent. It helped that Franklin come to be known as a rabid ebook collector and had an excellent series of his very personal, and so asking his opponent to lend him a e-book that he himself did not already very own become some problem of a flattery.

After this, the 2 have become buddies and he became Franklin's political enemy no more. But how did that take region? The concept behind this impact is that the thoughts tries to dictate and on the equal time rationalize actions. Franklin's opponent come to be already reason on doing Franklin this want and that motion of kindness skewed his perception that he did no longer like Franklin. To located it absolutely, he concept 'I am doing this man a choice therefore I need to actually like and apprehend this guy.'

This is each different tactic that can be used to sway human beings's evaluations that you may use any time. Try coming to a person with a huge or unreasonable request. Say you return to someone and ask them if they may run to the store for you and select you up a bag of flour. They will maximum in all likelihood refuse. Then go to them and decrease the request to virtually lending you a cup of flour, which grow to be all you desired inside the first location.

Chances are they will feel awful about spurning you the primary time and relent to granting you your greater low cost request. This individual has simply done you a prefer and the idea within the again of this intellectual manipulation tactic is that if you can get a person to do some thing for you as quickly as, it's far much less complex to get them to do some component for you yet again and shift their photo of you of their minds.

Again, human beings don't need to think that they may be performing some element to assist human beings they don't like and as soon as a choose is accomplished, it is easier for them to definitely convince themselves that they actually do like that man or woman.

Winning Favor

While Ben Franklin has now not been credited with the following techniques they may be consistent with his approach of triumphing over enemies and gaining prefer wherein there was none in advance than.

Have you ever heard the phrase imitation is the nice form of flattery? If so then you definitely definately are already familiar with the number one concept of mimicry and frame language can be used for manipulation. The idea is that whilst you mimic someone's gestures, idiosyncrasies and body language, you are paying them tribute. You are validating them and what they do and the way they act. This is a outstanding way to make yourself extra favorable in someone's eyes and cause them to more congenial to requests. They are greater inclined to look you as a person who "receives" or "is aware" them in preference to someone that they've to be on their protect round.

Leading the body language yourself is any other way to make someone extra open to particular requests. For instance, nodding masses at some stage in communique may be useful for getting a person to say positive to a positive preference. This is because of the fact human beings are simply at risk of imitation so while you nod lots as you are speakme and fundamental as heaps as a request, the individual you are speakme to will in all likelihood begin to nod as properly. This locations them in an agreeable mood due to the fact nodding is the acquainted movement of assent.

Embedded Commands

An embedded command is essentially a sentence that has been contrived steady with a additives for manipulation and NLP. Embedded instructions are a way to shift a subject's wondering within the path of a perception or educate of idea that is greater favorable to yours or one so as to bring about an very last consequences of your deciding on. Like subliminal and supraliminal messaging, the element is to get a person to act or enjoy a positive way without them understanding that they've been coaxed into feeling or appearing that way.

Embedded instructions are made of weasel phrases, command verbs, a state of being, way or experience, a commanding tone of voice after which the command itself. It is a selected technique with a view to make the situation plenty greater congenial to the command when you consider that it is the usage of presuppositions and it's miles being spoken to them in a tone that is neither bossy, nor passive. The trick is to country things as a rely of reality.

There is not something incorrect with mentioning topics as a depend of reality. The goal of embedded instructions is to blatantly command someone to perform a bit aspect without seeming like you are making a command in any respect. We normally have a tendency to talk with a passive tone while we ask a person to do some thing for us and at the same time as we're truly adamant about some element we will be predisposed to speak too brazenly.

The trick to embedded instructions is to find out a assured tone with out seeming too authoritative. For instance, exercising saying an obviously proper phrase time and again once more like, "the sky is blue." This is not a fake declaration in any regard and everyone is aware of that the sky is in truth blue. You can say this with complete self belief knowing that what you are pronouncing is universally popular because the truth.

Now try to say extraordinary matters that aren't as actual like "the sky is crimson" with the equal particular tone you used to say "the sky is blue." This will assist teach you to talk in a depend of fact tone this is vital for embedded commands. When you are saying "the sky is pink" don't inflect your tone upward like humans do at the same time as they may be asking a question or even as they're supplying an idea that appears incredulous. Keep a sincere, assured tone that is not overbearing or intrusive.

Once you've got mastered the commanding tonality it's time to move onto the following step...

Weasel Phrases

Weasel phrases are like getting your foot into the the the front door of your assignment's unconscious. They are important phrases that installation the command and can be commands in and of themselves. Consider them the top of the snake this is the complete embedded command. Weasel phrases are the beginnings of statements or questions that both presupposes that someone will feel a sure way, invitations them to undergo in thoughts a high-quality possibility, deflects motion onto any other metaphorical man or woman, gets rid of doubt that some component will take region or hides the command through telling someone that they shouldn't do some thing else.

Again, the weasel phrase is liable for putting in place the command and getting the individual proper right right into a inclined u . S .. One instance of a weasel announcement is one which sets up the rest of the command as a foregone surrender and presupposes that a person will act, assume or enjoy a positive way:

"As you start to..."

Notice how this weasel phrase gets rid of any doubt that a person will not do what the rest of the sentence instructions. It presupposes that the situation will act a extraordinary way and leaves no room for communicate.

Another example that deflects responsibility onto each distinct individual is:

"Someone can…"

In this enjoy you're disarming the state of affairs because of the reality you aren't speaking about them. You are speakme approximately "someone" else which may be a nice set up for an embedded command because the person does not assume for a minute that you are speaking about some component that they should do or revel in.

Command Verbs

The command verb is probably the most effective a part of the system as they may range counting on what your meant command is and can be switched out as desired. They are verbs that dictate an motion and serve to in addition lead the project down a course of susceptibility to command. Let's use the weasel phrases that we have got had been given already familiarized ourselves with and hyperlink them to command verbs:

"As you start to word..."

The command verb in this case is of route, word. We are telling the difficulty that they may perform a little issue with our weasel word "As you start to" after which we are telling them what that some element is with our command verb: study.

"Someone can dislike..."

In this situation you can be in search of to get someone to reveal toward a person else which would be a incredible case wherein to use the type of weasel word that deflects obligation onto a metaphorical man or woman because of the truth the problem can be averse to disliking a person themselves. Anyhow, the command verb right right here is dislike. Pretty clean, proper?

States, Processes and Experiences

States, approaches and studies are the following step inside the embedded command system. This is the part of the additives in which you can in reality make your command. Some examples of states are happiness, pride, elation, hatred, anger and frustration. Some examples of strategies include shifting, strolling, feeling, converting your ideals, softening your coronary coronary heart, being open minded and choosing a specific route. Some examples of reviews that artwork in this system are being afraid, getting excited, being brave or displaying reverence for.

This is essentially the beef and potatoes of your embedded command. You can use nice states, strategies and reminiscences to form the real command you need to carry. Let's whole the samples we've got got already laid out with commanding states, approaches or tales:

"As you begin to have a look at a softening of your coronary coronary coronary heart you may sense lots consolation."

In the above example, we used softening of the coronary coronary heart as our technique command. You may also moreover be aware that we brought a high nice feeling in regard to the command manner. This is completed to beautify the positivity of the command and spherical it out. But what about a command that isn't geared toward a high notable stop?

Again we're capable of use our hooked up sample for instance. Remember that in our "Someone can dislike..." instance we are attempting to reveal a person within the path of a person else:

"Someone can dislike a person for making them enjoy like much less of a human."

In this case we have got have been given used an revel in as our command in preference to a tool like we did within the previous instance. The enjoy we used end up feeling like much less of a human and it is a horrible reinforcement to go with the terrible command needed to reveal someone off of every other person.

At this element you have were given were given helped the individual disassociate themselves from the unsightly industrial corporation of turning towards someone in conjunction with your weasel phrase that assigns obligation for the act to someone else, implanted the command verb dislike to persuade them closer to the revel in command of feeling like less of a human and finished your embedded command, leaving your state of affairs to undergo in thoughts the manner a sure person may also additionally moreover have handled them in a stable manner and inclining them to dislike that sure individual.

Again the command tone you operate can be very important to the whole way. You want to typically be aware about the manner you're talking even as you're delivering your embedded command and continuously make sure that it's miles neither feeble nor too assertive, neither timid nor overbearing. Keep an incredible keel, exercise and devise a number of your very personal embedded instructions using the weasel phrase, command verb, revel in/kingdom/manner and command tonality machine.

Chapter 6: Charisma and Love Bombing

Manipulation comes in plenty of paperwork and can be deployed in nearly any state of affairs. In this financial disaster we are capable of bypass over a form of manipulation this is typically implemented in romantic relationships. This form of manipulation is known as love bombing. Love bombing is pretty a whole lot what it looks as if: bombarding someone with flattery and speak of affection and adoration.

The element is to weigh down someone with expressions of admiration which can be typically reserved for two human beings who have seemed every different and were together for a long time. The trouble will now not recognize what to do with those expressions if executed efficaciously.

One of the principle abilties in love bombing is much like the pattern interrupts that we referred to a couple of chapters within the past: confusion. The issue is to confuse the priority that allows you to't make heads or tails of the depth of this more youthful courting and are much an awful lot less possibly to apprehend that they may be in reality, being manipulated.

Another crucial element of a success love bombing is dependency. Over time, the affection bomber will nurture the challenge's dependence on them. This is important because while the problem feels that they will be the most effective character who can offer them with the tenderness and love that the love bomber has been copiously meting out to them, they will little by little start to flow into faraway from the opposite humans of their lives and location the manipulator on a better pedestal of precedence. Dependency furthermore heightens the nation of misunderstanding because of the truth as they waft far from aim observers they will be a bargain much less likely to be advised that they'll be being manipulated.

The motive that love bombing is this kind of effective tool for manipulation is that pretty a good deal all people wishes love and such some of people are searching out it. It is a fertile vicinity for manipulation and it may be very tough to hit upon besides the priority is a particularly cynical character – which might cause them to a lousy desire of task for this form of manipulation within the first vicinity.

But permit's say you have not chosen a difficult-nose cynic as your undertaking. Who's to mention that a person who's paying you an entire lot of compliments is making an attempt to govern you? I suggest, there are quality humans in the international right? Love bombing is a effective tool for manipulation because of the truth most people enjoy that they will be well worth of love and giving it to them (even though it's miles disingenuous) makes them malleable due to the truth they enjoy that they have finally found a few component unique.

You have likely heard of or seen examples of affection bombing to your very own existence. They typically come in the form of a dating shifting way too fast. Love bombing additionally may be used on more than one humans right away. Love bombing is truly a tactic that many cult leaders have used. They put in force a feeling of specialness in a set of people, inform them that they will be decided on, extraordinary or in any other case terrific from the rest of the arena. They feed on the feelings of inadequacy of a set of those who then emerge as the individual's fans.

It doesn't even need to be that overt, despite the fact that. Have you ever stated someone who had their boyfriend or lady friend cope with pretty a first-rate deal all in their issues for them? This is a conventional example of the dependence tactic embedded in love bombing. Once someone starts offevolved offevolved to rely upon someone else to cope with their difficult conditions for them, they find it more hard to anticipate their lives without that character.

As important as it's miles to understand a way to successfully execute love bombing to govern a person, it's far further vital to have the capability to inform at the equal time as someone is attempting to love bomb you. Fortunately, there are a few tell-story symptoms of love bombing:

Someone who is attempting to use the affection bomb tactic of manipulation will generally dig for facts on their trouble. In precise, they will want to understand masses about the awful topics which have happened interior the issue's lifestyles — annoying studies, awful romantic relationships, problems with their family, health problems, tribulations at work, insecurities and some thing horrible. If someone is constantly prodding you to inform them about the terrible factors of your existence it's miles a lifeless giveaway.

Love bombing consists of accelerating the natural go along with the go with the flow of emotions in a relationship so another manner you could encounter this tactic is by means of manner of taking have a look at if someone is telling you that they love you after excellent a couple weeks or a month of courting. They may additionally say that they realise it's far unexpected however that they count on they're falling for you or that they comprehend which you are the character they have been supposed to be with. Look out for phrases like "future" or "fate." A manipulator will use the ones illusory phrases to make you enjoy that your courting with them goes past you as people definitely so you'll be greater reluctant to really toss them aside.

A manipulator will also probably talk down special humans for your life. They do this because of the truth they want to make it appear that they're a exquisite man or woman. One way of attaining this lofty recognition in a topic's thoughts is through manner of debasing the alternative humans in a person's life. They could possibly ask approximately your pals and circle of relatives and discover strategies to pick out out at their flaws and factor out to you the strategies that they don't degree up. An smooth goal is ex-enthusiasts. Obviously it didn't workout for a few reason and a manipulator will ask you what that motive changed into – a regular sufficient question, right? They ought to likely begin comparing themselves to considered considered one of your exes in the appropriate regard of the cause you broke up with them.

A love bomber with a big bank account could probably buy you pretty a few gadgets. Materialism is a excellent manner to get someone addicted to you. If you have been seeing someone for only a few weeks and they have already sold you ornate items like jewelry, garments or electronics you could want to closely examine the validity of the connection. Remember that the point of affection bombing is to cram years' absolutely worth of romance into a few weeks so the whole thing can be improved even as someone is attempting to govern you with love bombing. If you sense that matters are going too rapid every physical or emotionally, a person can be trying to control you.

Using Charisma for Manipulation

Charisma is some component that is often spoken of in terms of "you're every born with it otherwise you're no longer." This is a misrepresentation of what air of secrecy truly is. Charisma is the capability to endear yourself to certainly one of a type humans in any manner form or shape. When you observe charism via this lens, the possibilities appear nearly countless.

There are myriad techniques that you can endear yourself to an character or perhaps a set of human beings. A ideal instance of this air of mystery on name for tactic is Steve Jobs. Steve Jobs became called a tremendous public speaker and someone who commanded a experience of awe at the same time as he entered a room. Jobs changed into charismatic and the manner one in each of his friends located it grow to be that Jobs wielded a "truth distortion difficulty."

This term comes from a Star Trek episode in which the Enterprise organization stumble upon a race of aliens which might be capable of create "fact distortion fields" through which they were able to embed false realities into the brains of their victims – essentially making them expect and accept as proper with that some thing has befell even as it surely hasn't.

Jobs became capable of provoke hundreds of human beings because of the reality he was capable of make them agree with in the impossible. He turn out to be able to make the people he spoke to adopt his dream and his imaginative and prescient as even though it were their very own.

This is a shape of aura that all of us is capable of. You definitely have to understand the techniques. For instance, folks that are appeared as charismatic often talk on their very own opinions, beliefs or accomplishments with tremendous enthusiasm and ardour. In order to implant your will into a person's mind you have to make it look like the assets you are pronouncing are worthwhile. This is step one and you could implement it with the resource of manner of speakme to someone about your ideals or critiques as despite the fact that hatching them come to be motive for party in and of itself.

Charisma is regularly related to self assurance and there is a cause for that — why may also want to truely everyone be willing to follow or bend to the selection of a person who sounds as despite the fact that they don't consider the words which can be popping out of their private mouths? You will in no way concentrate the most charismatic leaders of the world, past or gift, speakme timidly. You will in no manner concentrate them speak without steel assurance. You will in no way pay hobby them speaking as though they didn't consider that they knew what have become right and what changed into outstanding. Manipulators comprehend this tactic properly. They will communicate as though they recognize the whole lot, no matter the truth that they don't. In order to collect your non-public air of thriller, you need to attempt speaking in a assured manner even if the hassle depend isn't always some problem you're familiar with. Talk as in case you apprehend the whole lot approximately the challenge and those will begin to doubt themselves in mild of someone who speaks so with a bit of luck.

Another way you could boost your popularity in someone's mind and installation aura is with the resource of the use of evaluating yourself with a determine of recognize or admiration. Try talking about a modern-day-day trial or tribulation that you went through. Maybe some aspect to your private or professional life didn't skip the way you desired it to. This is a brilliant possibility to reveal your disasters into perceived successes and to perform that; you can truly examine your issues to a famous or pretty-appeared character who moreover suffered similar screw ups. For example, you could communicate about an example in which you acquire proper right here up quick on your expectations and then say a few element like "But rather, even Kobe Bryant didn't win as many jewelry as he desired." This is a totally diffused way of setting your self on the same plane as a a fulfillment or properly-respected individual.

There are specific approaches you can exercising developing your air of mystery in ordinary conversations as well:

Solid eye touch suggests that you are interested by what someone has to mention and gives you an appealing presence. Eye contact is an paintings, in spite of the fact that and it wants to be practiced as a way to be mastered. Too heaps can seem creepy and too little will make it seem as no matter the truth which you're uninterested and no longer present. Practice in regular situations like talking for your cashier on the grocery preserve or with a waiter at a eating place. Start via the use of keeping eye touch for without a doubt one 2nd longer than you commonly may and notice how the man or woman reacts. You may be able to gage any ache if it's far too prolonged. But if the individual does not cringe, strive maintaining it for a chunk longer.

Speaking slowly and with cause is each one of a kind accurate manner to command interest and apprehend. People often attempt to rush their phrases out to get their element throughout as quick as feasible however that cheapens the price of what they may be pronouncing. By speakme slowly and intentionally, people will understand what you are saying with substance and significance.

Body language goes a protracted way in growing charisma. Words can only accomplish that a remarkable deal so humans appearance to the manner which you skip as a validation which you are taking note of them and whilst you communicate, which you are speaking with conviction. Accentuating factors on the same time as you're talking with a hand gesture is an instance of extremely good body language. Smiling is any other. You also can attempt furrowing your brow or frowning while a person is telling you a sad or lousy story. When someone is announcing some thing this is manifestly critical to them, strive leaning in a hint to expose them which you are listening and that you trust them on the significance of the concern to the factor which you don't need to miss a phrase. Good posture is huge for developing charisma too. Keep your again instantly but don't over-straighten. Keeping the shoulders unfastened and the again straight away is a remarkable region to start.

Chapter 7: Combining Charisma with the Love Bomb Technique

The cause why we're talking about air of secrecy in the identical financial disaster because the affection bombing approach is due to the fact when you have charisma, love bombing will become plenty less difficult toward the ends of manipulation and developing have an impact on over a person. When worked out in tandem, charismatic love bombing becomes a wonderful device for manage.

Now that you recognize the methods in which you could growth air of mystery you could begin considering procedures to location it to paintings thru love bombing. We mentioned flattery and the manner it pertains to love bombing because of the fact it's miles an crucial step in the direction of gaining impact over a person. The pleasant shape of flattery is sincere flattery. If there's a few element that you absolutely rate or admire about someone – it can be the manner they do their hair, their style revel in, their voice, the manner they make a fine gesture or some thing like that – make it a issue to permit that man or woman comprehend and don't allow them to miss it. This is the proper manner to use flattery efficaciously because of the fact you may no longer need to set up any more attempt in making it seem actual and protecting your right intentions. But there are special strategies.

If you truly can't take into account a detail which you actually respect approximately a person, pass the possibility direction: play on their insecurities. One of the fastest strategies to endear your self to someone is thru reading what they will be insecure about and building them up in that regard. For example, in case your trouble is shy about smiling then they may be likely self-conscious about their enamel. You have positioned your in. If their teeth are crooked, tell them you're surprised at how white they're. If they will be yellow, tell them you desire you had enamel as at once as theirs. If their tooth are crooked and yellow tell them that it gives them man or woman and that a number of the maximum well-known and loved people like Freddie Mercury had masses lots much less than amazing teeth.

Complimenting people in a set is a very powerful manner to make certain that reward sticks with the man or woman both consciously and subconsciously. When unique people can concentrate, release a compliment at your problem. You gets the most bang on your reward dollar at the identical time as there are outstanding humans spherical to concentrate it.

We moreover mentioned dependency in this financial disaster, however how do you create dependency? Dependency may be generated in a pair notable methods however the stylish idea in the back of nurturing dependence is to set up your self as a person of importance to the concern as plenty as you in all likelihood can. You can try this through showering the assignment with flattery and making your self available for them to talk to at any time. Many human beings are in need of human beings to be aware of them so making your self to be had to talk all the time is a exquisite manner to nurture dependence. Once you have were given have been given set up your self as your venture's flow-to when they want a sympathetic ear (see how frame language, eye touch and different factors of air of mystery can weave seamlessly via love bombing techniques?) they may begin to rely on you for this act of affection.

If someone feels that no person treats them with the kindness, tenderness and reward which you do then they'll be heaps more reluctant to provide you up. They turns into counting on you to reinforce their self guarantee and provide kind words to them. Showering a subject with compliments will make you a safe haven to run to at the same time as they are feeling low. Soon they'll come to be so related to you for that reason that they may be inclined to do something it takes to maintain this organized alternate of emotion and encouragement.

Handling everyday duties and hard conditions is each other way to broaden dependence. Be there to your scenario once they get a flat tire or assist them with grocery shopping. The greater you do, large or small, the greater they it's going to probably be normalized inside the thoughts of the situation and the greater they will come to rely upon you because the person to assist them out of a jam.

We touched on the thoughts of future and future as they pertain to love bombing, but permit's get into the specifics and the way you could use it on your advantage. The mind of destiny and future make the relationship seem grander than it in reality is. They serve to in addition romanticize the concept of being with you and are consequently very beneficial in terms of manipulation. When you inform a person that you feel like "you have been supposed to be together" or "I realize you are the only one for me" they start to be a part of a more significance to their association with you. They might not remember it inside the beginning but in case you are regular with it and adamant approximately your perception their partitions will in the long run come tumbling down.

Try slowly putting it into the conversations you have on the side of your mission. "You might imagine I'm loopy, however I'm beginning to feel a kinship with you that I've by no means had with all and sundry else" is a fantastic one, so is "I experience such as you and I had been imagined to discover each distinctive." The task may additionally moreover moreover snort the ones declarations of future off on the begin but if you are constant with them they'll slowly start to agree with you to be honest. Once they begin to entertain the sincerity of your feelings, they'll start to consider your grandiose thoughts as fact.

Dark NLP Technique four: 5 Powerful Manipulation Tactics

In this financial ruin we're able to bypass over 5 traditional and powerful techniques for mental manipulation. These strategies require subtlety, as they play on the base feelings of someone collectively with fear and doubt. Being too overt with any of the subsequent strategies should bring about draw back or disconnect – the trouble can also start to recognize your cause and paintings to sever ties with you.

So finesse is the call of the game with these and most of the processes we've were given mentioned up to now. Subtlety and patience are the splendid mask for the following strategies. Some of them take time and they all require a delicate touch. Sometimes manipulation can be like gardening: you sow the seeds, expect them to sprout and you then definately gently nurture the growth. Keep this in thoughts as you move over the ones five manipulation techniques.

Gaslighting

The term gaslighting comes from a 1940 film in which the protagonist's husband begins to make her doubt her personal sanity through dimming the fuel lighting fixtures in her rental. When she questions him as to whether or not he thinks the lights appearance dimmer, he says no. He maintains frequently (we see endurance at play) dimming the lights however does not admit that they are any dimmer.

The motive of gaslighting is to make the difficulty doubt themselves on a sure problem. It might be a few component from lights in an apartment to the colour in their hair. It is a way designed to instill a form of dependence – the problem will begin to query themselves on a couple of fronts and turn to the manipulator as their supply of fact and unity. Once the manipulator is in this feature, she or he has a number of sway in how the situation thinks and acts.

Imagine for a minute in case you couldn't consider your private memory. You may additionally look to a person else that will help you keep in mind subjects, right? Imagine that intellectual country of no longer being capable of rely on your self for a primary feature. You could possibly feel helpless, insecure and in determined want of a helping hand. You may additionally also be willing to sacrifice masses for that helping hand.

That mental united states of america you in reality imagined is the intention of gaslighting. The act of gaslighting is simply pretty easy, conceptually. All it takes is to instill some doubt in a person's head. But the workout of it could take some being used to.

One instance of gaslighting consists of countering a perception that the hassle has. For instance, allow's say your assignment recollects some thing that came about at a party. You should say a few thing like "Wait, that's no longer in truth the manner it took place."

In this case you're countering the validity of a memory with some exceptional model of truth. You can skip on with this situation via manner of presenting a few other version (a fake one) of what passed off at said birthday party.

Another method of gaslighting is diversion. For instance, allow's say the priority is bringing up some thing you can have completed in the past. You should use diversion and reply with, "There goes your over-lively imagination once more."

In this situation the manipulator is diverting the truth through the lens that the task is truly imagining topics – basically belittling the trouble's ideals.

Repetition is a sneaky manner to instill doubt in someone's mind. When someone makes a assertion about a few component, the usage of repetition might sound a few thing like this: "Are you satisfactory?! Are you truely superb about that?!"

Questioning someone at each opportunity will make them doubt themselves finally if they accept as real with that what they'll be pronouncing sounds incredulous to you.

You might also even enlist unique occasions for gaslighting. One powerful manner of making someone doubt themselves is telling them that considered one of a type humans take into account a few factor counter to their beliefs. For example, allow's say your assignment believes that he's a quite particular athlete. You can gaslight him via saying a few issue to the effect of "You recognise there are quite a few people at the health club who don't truely like having you at the team even as we play basketball. They simply don't need to harm your emotions."

Planting phantom ideals supposedly held through others is however every other effective way to get a person to start doubting themselves. And there you've got it - gaslighting is a dark tool of manipulation and deceit that manipulators but use to terrific impact.

Playing the Victim and Using Guilt

Playing the victim can be an remarkable way to get what you need in case you are willing to portray your self in a miles an awful lot less than favorable mild. Many human beings use the victim function as a way to get different human beings to do things for them. On a grander scale, gambling the victim is a totally awesome approach to maintain immediately to a partner or massive distinct.

You should word that the sufferer tactic want to not be overused if it is to be powerful, but. That's because of the truth humans is probably loads an awful lot much less inclined to do subjects for you if you are constantly playing the victim role. Instead, you should observe this approach as form of a closing-ditch or an emergency method of manipulation for at the same time as you actually need or want a few aspect.

So playing the sufferer includes one or all of the following: gambling dumb, making your self appear sheepish and/or making it appear that the area is continuously beating you down. For example, one may probably play dumb so that you could make themselves the sufferer with the resource of announcing some factor like "I simply don't recognize why I can't get in advance." It's a quite clean device sincerely — truly begin with an ignorant announcement and forestall it with a grandiose declaration about your lifestyles.

Another instance may be, "I can't figure out what is making me so unpopular."

In the above instance, "I can't determine out what..." is the statement of lack of know-how and "is making me so unpopular" is the grandiose life statement.

Making your self look sheepish is essentially getting human beings to endure in thoughts that you are constantly getting the short stop of the stick. It includes making yourself look willing and pathetic. You are essentially debasing yourself. Let's say you are trying to get a beautify or a advertising and marketing and marketing at art work. Your boss denies your face-to-face request but you want to use the victim tactic to get him to trade his thoughts. You can also want to make yourself seem sheepish through announcing "Yeah that's what I figured. I continuously get handed up for promotions/increases. I'm now not even excessive first-class why I ."

This also can make your boss feel sorry for you. If so you then clearly have efficaciously manipulated your boss into imparting you with a enhance/merchandising with the victim tactic.

The sufferer function may be efficiently discovered by means of using way of tugging at the coronary coronary heart strings of the hassle. For example, allow's say you're asking your problem for some of their lunch. They refuse to that you reply "Probably for the remarkable, I must stand to shed kilos except."

This is an instance of gambling the victim by means of the usage of making it appear to be the arena is constantly towards you. You are hungry, you may't get food and on pinnacle of all that, you are fats.

Playing the victim rolls well into the guilt difficulty of manipulation. Once you've got were given installed yourself due to the fact the victim, you can take it a step in addition with the aid of way of making someone feel guilty. Guilting someone into doing a little element for you is a commonplace form of manipulation. For example, permit's say you need your remarkable exclusive to take you somewhere and are reluctant. You can nudge them via announcing "But you in no manner take me everywhere."

Another scenario: you want your project that will help you flow. You can guilt them into doing it with the useful resource of bringing up an instance in which you helped them. "Remember that point I gave you a adventure to paintings on the identical time as your vehicle modified into damaged down?"

Both of these guilting examples play on someone's propensity to revel in awful about the beyond. If you observe, these examples and maximum awesome examples of guilt, deliver up something approximately the beyond. Still, not anyone is liable to feeling responsible. Therefore the guilt tactic must be launched cautiously upon a person is liable to feelings of guilt.

Chapter 8: Inspire Fear, then Relief

The fear/remedy tactic of manipulation is one that is predicated on each other intellectual mechanic we referred to in beyond chapters: confusion/disarming. The worry/remedy technique of manipulation is quite a unusual highbrow phenomenon. Studies have proven that once human beings are disarmed and in a kingdom of mild confusion they're more congenial to requests.

So superb, the concern/remedy technique of manipulation can be used to get someone to offer you some element or act favorably towards you in some experience. The fear then treatment tactic consists of instilling some form of fear into a person and then relieving them that there may be honestly no purpose to be afraid. After their fears had been allayed the manipulator will then make a few sort of request to which the mission might be much more likely to answer sincerely to.

You have truely seen this 'suitable cop horrible cop' tactic in movement on TV and in movies when police officers are interrogating a suspect. There is constantly an average cop who threatens the suspect with violence or an extended jail sentence and then there may be a nice cop who offers a sympathetic shoulder and assures the suspect that he'll do some thing it takes to help her or him out.

This is mental manipulation inside the path of getting the priority to cooperate with interrogators. In essence, the problem opinions a deep and sudden mood swing in quick succession: an abrupt rush of fear followed with the useful resource of remedy. This brief change in intellectual moods is what confuses and disarms the state of affairs — making them more likely to act irrationally or to do some issue they usually wouldn't. The phenomenon is similar to giving a nonsensical strategy to a ordinary question like we said in beyond chapters. It locations the character right into a country of misunderstanding.

That is also the reason with the concern/consolation tactic. You can rent this shape of manipulation pretty outcomes and in normal situations. For example, let's say you're in the car together with your hassle and then you definitely point out that you are paying attention to a bizarre sound coming from the engine. The hassle doesn't pay interest something (due to the reality the sound is fictitious) but they're proper now conquer with dread that their vehicle goes to interrupt down or that they may brief be dealing with a hefty mechanic invoice. You look ahead to a bit at the same time as the hassle is cautiously listening to the sound of their engine and then you definately definately definately say, "Oh wait that was in truth the auto inside the lane subsequent to us. Hey, do you thoughts dropping me off on the economic institution?"

This is assuming that the goal of the manipulator changed into to get the concern to provide them a ride to the bank however you may update the request with pretty an awful lot a few element. In this situation, the trouble can be more willing to grant a preference because they may be relieved that there can be honestly nothing incorrect with their car. It's like doing the situation a opt for, but now not certainly. Imagine worry/remedy like this: solving a hassle which you created and that during no way existed inside the first vicinity.

You want to make the man or woman get hold of as actual with that their fear is based absolutely in fact in order that they may really enjoy that you lifted a weight off in their shoulders through presenting them with the solution – or remedy – to their fears. You can create any phantom fear. To provide you with some different instance, say you want your problem to babysit your children over the weekend. You are in their residence and then you definitely actually definitely say which you scent some element awesome...a few aspect that smells like mould. You say "No I've smelled this in advance than in my vintage condominium. That is surely the scent of mold." Then you sniff round similarly to analyze and then you definately get to the waste basket and say, "Never mind it modified into in reality some issue is for your waste basket. That jogs my memory, are you able to babysit the youngsters this weekend?"

The worry of getting inhaled mould for who is aware of how long and then having to pay a person to get rid of it locations the scenario in a country of close to-panic. Then even as you understand it turned into the trash all along, they may be right away relieved and satisfied to furnish a request.

Following Unreasonable Requests with Reasonable ones

This technique of manipulation includes protecting your proper desire with a dummy one. In this technique you will pick out out some issue you want. It may be some aspect from a select to the jacket off the issue's lower back. But earlier than you ask the problem for this need you preface it with an unreasonable request.

This over again is type of like setting a phantom worry into the thoughts of the scenario and then playing the hero of dispelling this fake fear. In which case, they may be greater apt to reward you in your "company" via announcing tremendous to some thing you ask them.

In this example the fear is having to every grant or say no to an unreasonable or lofty request. Then while you relent and ask for something smaller (your actual desire inside the first area), they are relieved and more congenial in your request.

To give you an instance, don't forget if you can which you want to borrow $20 from your friend. This is a very easy instance and an easy way to launch the unreasonable/reasonably-priced tactic of manipulation. You say, "Could you lend me $one hundred fifty? I am in a actual tight jam." A lot of cash counting on who you communicate to so that you can tweak this situation therefore. The problem replies, "No that's an excessive amount of cash." Then you backtrack and nation your real request via saying, "Fine then are you capable of at least spare $20?" $20 is a much extra reasonable request so the hassle can be more likely to present you this meager loan. $20 is all you preferred inside the first place despite the fact that. You masked your actual choice thru a fake and over-inflated one.

This is the basis of the unreasonable/affordable request approach of manipulation. Again, it plays at the guilt of the priority. They can also moreover enjoy so terrible that they aren't able to supply your initial request (your fake and unreasonable one) that they will be determined to ease their accountable aware via supporting you in some smaller manner (your real and further low priced request).

Let's take a look at every special example of this tactic in movement. Assume that you have 4 friends flying in from out of nation but you can't located them up at your private home. But you have had been given a pal with 2 spare bedrooms of their house. You can be able to get them to put your buddies up thru falsifying the quantity of human beings which may be traveling. The communication may additionally moreover drift "Hey I actually have 8 pals traveling from out of u.S. And I come to be questioning if they might crash at your vicinity." Your trouble could possibly respond "eight people is lots, I don't assume I can do this." Then you reply with "Man I don't comprehend what to do. They need a place to live. Ok how approximately four of them live at my region and 4 live at yours?"

In this case you're the usage of guilt coupled with the lower priced/unreasonable request tactic as a way to get your pal to residence your internet site traffic. The task in this case will feel horrific approximately not helping you out and then be relieved at the same time as you scale back your request to a extra affordable one. In case you have got been questioning, this case ends with the mission saying "Ok."

Boundary Testing and Psychological Conditioning

Boundary attempting out and mental conditioning are the prolonged-con version of manipulation. With this tactic, you're finding out the waters of what your challenge will tolerate through the years. This is a high instance of a manipulation tactic that takes time and finesse. If you go overboard too quick, the priority can be repellant and entice on on your pastime. But if you are affected man or woman and mood your phrases and/or actions, you will draw the problem out slowly –priming them for extended-term manipulation.

This tactic dictates that you gently push the bounds of what your challenge will get hold of. Little via little the ones barriers will expand. This situations the hassle to clearly take transport of more and more. It is shape of like how an prolonged-distance runner will teach themselves by first strolling one mile, then two, then 3 and so forth. Their body will become greater capable of tolerate the rigors of the distances. The mind works in the same way. A hassle may be capable of tolerate greater if you train them to.

Let's recall an instance that you may be capable of use at paintings. Say your cause is to slowly but really divert extra of your art work to a person else so that in the end, you do little to no artwork the least bit. You can start via the usage of the usage of asking your coworker to kind up just half of of your file because of the truth you are without a doubt pressed with other topics. If they receive you then have your venture. Don't push it too a long way. Wait a few days or in keeping with week before your subsequent request however make it a bit huge. Ask them to cope with the entire record.

At this thing they will be already primed (this is additionally known as the "foot-in-the-door" technique of manipulation) due to this that because they already completed one need for you, they may be more likely to carry out each unique. You keep this over a matter of months till in the end you have someone else managing all of your reviews.

Of route this approach may be used for almost any detail of life. For example you can psychologically scenario someone into wondering it's absolutely high-quality which you come over for dinner 3 nights in line with week through way of way of commencing sluggish and inquiring for that they feed you one night according to week. Then 2 nights, then 3 and so forth and so on.

Again, the critical factor to this tactic is staying power and finesse so don't soar the gun and make your requests too close to in succession. Space them out and begin them off very reasonably. Over time your challenge can be unwittingly educated to provide in for your requests irrespective of how massive.

Dark NLP Technique 6: Framing as a Powerful Tool

In this economic catastrophe we can call upon most of the classes we've placed out about hypnosis from preceding chapters. This financial catastrophe offers with conversational hypnosis. Conversational hypnosis is a manner to consciously manage your challenge with out all of the theatrics and drama of conventional hypnosis. So sure, it's miles however a few other covert approach of manipulation wherein, if performed efficiently, the challenge will don't have any consciousness of the manipulation taking location.

In order to effectively install conversational hypnosis and use it on your benefit, you will need to find out about a concept referred to as framing.

What are Frames in Hypnosis?

To located it in base phrases, frames are context. Frames are used every day in casual conversation however simplest the professional manipulators and darkish NLP practitioners use them to any avail. When you're speaking to definitely everybody approximately some thing there is a body round that conversation – a context.

Frames generally come from someone's personal ideals, how they view themselves and the way they view the location. To put it a few exceptional manner, frames are in fact how we view the sector or a sure trouble depend number.

In hypnosis, we use the ones contexts to form the mind and reviews of our topics. Frames are a manner to govern the conversations and their outcomes.

For instance: you're having a communique in conjunction with your friend about giving exchange to the homeless. Your pal says some thing to the effect of "I don't do it because of the reality they simply purchase booze." To which you reply and exchange the body of the conversation thru asserting, "Most homeless are veterans who fought for our u.S.A.."

Chapter 9: Four Frames you Can Manipulate

Now that you have an concept of what a conversational body is you may find out approximately the four one-of-a-type frames. These four frames can all be used to manipulate your problem. They encompass the preframe, keeping body, reframe and the deframe.

In order to maintain your frame you could call upon a number of the attention-touch bodily video games we cited in preceding chapters. Maintaining your frame is all approximately being an immovable item. Maintaining a frame approach not letting each person else alternate a given frame.

If you need to hold a frame or context in a communique and not permit or not it's far shifted you want to deliver no credit score to truely anybody else's body. You can do this via preserving cause eye touch without reacting to the terms or recommendations of the difficulty. Say you are ordering meals together with your mission and that they issue out that they enjoy like fowl. Without skipping a beat you look them useless in the eye and say "The turkey here is sudden." By no longer acknowledging some issue they said approximately bird and giving an instantaneous and cause statement about the turkey you have got were given maintained the body on turkey being favorable.

Preframing includes cautious consideration of all outcomes. If you need someone to walk out on their boyfriend you may preframe via the usage of first questioning what it'd take for a girl to stroll out on their boyfriend. Maybe the boyfriend cheated. Preframing will make it so the issue thinks there's no exclusive logical cause for his or her boyfriend's conduct other than he cheated.

Reframing includes shifting a person's body on a given problem altogether. This is finished through offering an alternate view of whatever the difficulty is. Bringing up quality matters (right or now not) about some factor your situation perspectives negatively may be an powerful manner to reframe.

Deframing is used at the same time as someone is tough a body you are attempting to impose. In it, as opposed to protecting your body or stance, you could solution their challenge with a undertaking to their frame. This flips the table and pts the state of affairs returned on the safety in which they want to be.

How to Maintain your Frame in Conversational Hypnosis

Maintaining a frame may be difficult for some people because of the fact it may imply exuding an entire lot of charisma and self notion. This is why eye-contact practice is so important due to the truth steady and cause eye-contact is one of the best strategies to maintain frame. When a person isn't breaking their gaze with you on the same time as speaking, that act by myself puts a heavier weight on their terms.

In addition to eye-contact, a self-self perception that what you're pronouncing is the most crucial reality presently being cited allows pretty. You don't have to break a person at the same time as they may be speakme. Let them talk and whilst they will be finished, honestly keep taking region your frame as despite the fact that they in no manner said a few element.

Let's check how one may hold their frame. In the following example, the manipulator is "A" and the difficulty is "B."

A: Nothing in this worldwide is better than making love

B: What about own family and pals?

A: Making love is what connects us to truly being human and is therefore crucial

B: I'm not positive if that's right

A: Making love is the high-quality natural trouble in the global. It's grand, it's holy, it's historical it's godly

B: I count on assisting others is all of those subjects

A: Nothing on this international is higher than making love

You see how "A" in no way even considered B's assertions and did not answer B's question. It changed into nearly like A have become having a communique collectively collectively with his or herself. A have become preoccupied along along with his/her perception due to the truth that that they had ideally fitted self assure in it due to the fact the most crucial fact. Therefore, they could not be veered a ways from it.

The purpose of maintaining body is to provide your frame so optimistically that the situation has no preference however to question their very very own ideals inside the incessant slight of your very very own.

How to Use Preframing in Conversational Hypnosis

Preframing is like priming a topic to bend to your will. Reframing includes cautiously considering the ability doubts and objections that a topic may also have collectively together with your very very very own body or will. The concept is to get their minds set on some thing aside from their real objections.

Say you need to get a black fridge for your house but you recognize that your roommate goals a silver one. You can preframe your roommate thru mentioning that the silver fridge they want doesn't have sufficient garage area even if you recognize it does.

Bombard them with all of the matters they received't be capable of shop inside the silver one; watermelons, entire chickens, meal prep Tupperware, soda, beer, blocks of cheese, gallons of milk. This gets their minds on the non-existent problem of the silver refrigerator now not having enough garage region. Then you may implant the concept of the black refrigerator. The colour of the fridge isn't loads of a problem anymore now that their mind is going off on a tangent of storage capability rather than colour.

The key to preframing is knowing what your trouble's frame is. You will need to realize what they may be concerned about, what their doubts are and what they accept as actual with to be actual. Then you need to counter the ones beliefs and concerns by way of converting them with others. The real fear or trouble desires to wander away for a chunk on the same time as you implant your will.

How to Use Reframing in Conversational Hypnosis

As we touched on earlier, reframing is basically converting a person's mind about some problem. It is all approximately getting a topic to look a few component in a one in all a type moderate. We can do this via the use of attaching new that means to something that already has a hard and fast which means in a person's mind.

The first step in reframing someone is to apprehend exactly how they enjoy about a pleasant trouble count variety. The next step is to both stable doubt on that belief or to give that notion in a ultra-modern slight. The final step in reframing is to beautify this new perspective.

Let's say as an example that your task hates the idea of going to the dentist. You understand that they hate the dentist which is essentially step one in reframing but it permits to understand exactly why they hate the dentist. What is it approximately the dentist that makes your problem recoil? Do they have got any lousy beyond research with the dentist? These are questions you could want to have replied as they'll help you reframe.

Assume which you understand that the drills dentists use are why your situation doesn't like going. So the communique may match some aspect like this:

"I hate the dentist"

"You recognize there are masses of human beings in precise nations who may kill to visit the dentist"

"I recognize however I can't stand the drills"

"Most dentists use modern drills that get the approach finished a bargain extra quick and quietly and without a ache"

"I truely although don't like going"

"You understand dentists nowadays are expert in particular to ease the tensions in their patients. Regular dental visits are the first-rate problem that will help you hold your teeth healthful and handsome too"

"That appears suitable"

In this case you're dropping a brand new mild and perspective on going to the dentist. You point out underprivileged human beings and modern-day dental techniques to shed a state-of-the-art light.

Then you beef up the idea with the aid of using using citing the fitness and appearance of the trouble's teeth.

After strolling via all of the steps of reframing (being acquainted with the fears of the problem, losing a new moderate on that fear and riding the issue home) the hassle relents and starts offevolved to shift their thinking. The stuff approximately the drills and the education won't additionally be right!

How to Use Deframing in Conversational Hypnosis

Deframing is getting a person to do what you want thru challenging their non-public body rather than simply in search of to alternate or adjust it. Like body retaining it includes instilling a seed of doubt to your situation's head however in contrast to border retaining you use worrying situations in choice to sheer, unwavering self guarantee.

Deframing may be used in conversational hypnosis mainly if a person is thinking your very personal frame. The first step in deframing is to no longer answer the selection to protect your frame. Ignore the wondering like you probable did even as you have got been strolling on frame maintaining.

The 2d step is without a doubt to impeach why it's far that the venture believes what they remember. It is essential to not query the cause they'll be challenging you due to the reality this may be an acknowledgement of that line of wondering. We don't want to do this. Remember the motive is to disregard the assignment outright so don't even famend it. Instead, pass back to their base frame of perception and venture that.

This tactic takes some gumption and fortitude. You will need to be persistent because of the fact the more you question their middle ideals the more they'll be on the protecting and begin to question them themselves.

Let's say you don't recycle and your friend does. The verbal exchange might cross:

"You don't recycle due to the truth you don't care approximately the earth"

"Why is it which you recycle?"

At this point you've got overlooked the difficulty's invitation to debate their accusation which you don't care about the earth and characteristic efficiently carried out the first step in deframing.

"Because now not such as you, I care approximately our planet"

"Do you in fact care about the planet?"

Here you have were given carried out step 2. You have successfully taken yourself out of the brand new seat and located your issue on the protective. Now they're answering your questions in place of the alternative manner round. Then, via asking in the event that they in truth care approximately the planet, you have got got questioned their center ideals.

"Of route I do"

"Do you clearly, or do you truely recycle to make it appear like you care?"

Now you've got got your issue on the ropes. They are answering your questions and characteristic absolutely given up on interrogating you as to why you don't recycle. You can cross on and on with this vein of thinking till your task starts to impeach themselves. You have effectively deframed them. You have the better hand. You are in the using pressure's seat and you've taken control of the verbal exchange and in all likelihood even modified what the issue believes.

Dark NLP Technique 7: Advanced Techniques and Suggestibility Testing

At this detail we've observed approximately numerous techniques of manipulation thru neuro-linguistic programming and hypnosis. By now you are armed with a plethora of weapons to use on any given situation, and you are organized defensively if a person tries to apply any of these processes in opposition to you. In this chapter, we are capable of pass over a pair of recent subjects that aren't manipulation techniques in and of themselves – they'll be although essential for understanding upon whom to put in the ones strategies on and for the safety of the manipulator.

Chapter 10: Suggestibility Testing

Many hypnotists will allow you to know that suggestibility trying out is awesome left to the street performers and leisure hypnotists. This may be real as it has restrained viability in hypnotherapy however what many hypnotists don't bear in mind is normal manipulation. Suggestibility trying out is massively utilizable within the realm of conversational hypnosis and regular hypnosis in the direction of the ends of manipulation. So what it's far?

Suggestibility trying out can talk over with any variety of verbal or physical "feelers" that assist the hypnotist decide whether or not or now not their situation is a exquisite purpose for hypnosis and manipulation. They can serve as a manual for one to decide how likely a subject will bend to their will. Some hypnotists use suggestibility training to determine how deep right right into a hypnotic trance their subjects are however our features could be a piece one in every of a type.

For our intents and capabilities we're able to use suggestibility finding out to discover our subjects in the first location. The purpose every person may want to use suggestibility finding out is to find out the proper hassle for manipulation. The caveat with hypnotism, even conversational hypnosis, is that a few people are extra suggestible to others. In different phrases, a few humans are a whole lot much less probably to be inducted into hypnosis than others. For this cause Dark NLP practitioners regularly use suggestibility finding out to have a better idea of who they might manage and who they may not be capable of.

The reason you could need to study those assessments is basically for average performance. For instance, you wouldn't want to use some of your effort and time searching for to govern a person whom you've examined to have low suggestibility. It need to in reality take too lengthy and besides, there are lots of with out problems suggestible desires to pick from. In reality, it's miles expected that as a bargain as eighty% of the populace is inside the commonplace style of hypnotic suggestibility – that means that as a whole lot as 80% of the population may be successfully hypnotized with slight try.

That is why suggestibility finding out is so beneficial for the Dark NLP practitioner. It gives a great guideline on who a top undertaking is probably and helps the practitioner avoid tough subjects.

Suggestibility tests can be deployed pretty with out problems. In most times you want to attempt at least the kind of checks earlier than you attempt the usage of any of the tactics we've got have been given mentioned to this point. Let's test some of the excellent strategies for trying out suggestibility.

The Light/Heavy Hands Technique

This approach of suggestibility attempting out is based upon intently on the attention and that imagination of the task. How keenly someone can deliver their awareness and creativeness into alignment is a completely crucial element. It will determine how inclined they'll be to actual hypnotic concept.

In this take a look at you may be capable of see a bodily manifestation of their degree of perception. It is every now and then known as the e-book and balloon take a look at as well and you could see why in just a moment. The concept in the back of this test is to look simply how deeply you'll be able to delve into their very own minds. The perception is that the body will react bodily if someone is specializing in some factor that they don't forget is actual. If you notice that your assignment reacts physical to the mild/heavy palms method then they're more than likely a top goal for Dark NLP and hypnosis. So right proper right here is what you'll need to do:

Ask someone, or a couple of humans, to shut their eyes and maintain their palms immediately out inside the the front of them. Tell them to have one hand grew to emerge as palm-as an entire lot due to the fact the sky and one hand palm-all of the way right right down to the floor. Now tell them to anticipate that in the hand that is going via within the path of the sky, they are carrying a watermelon. In the hand they've got coping with the floor, inform them that there are a collection of helium balloons tied to their wrist.

Go into detail about the watermelon. They can heady scent it, experience its rind and most significantly, enjoy how heavy it is. With each passing second their hands are becoming an increasing number of fatigued from the weight of the heavy watermelon. Meanwhile the arm with the balloons tied to it's far getting lighter because of the truth the balloons are slowly and lightly ascending inside the path of the sky. What you need to be doing on the same time as their eyes are closed is seeing if their arms are truely transferring. If they'll be, then you definately absolutely've maximum in all likelihood determined your problem.

The Amnesia Technique

The amnesia approach is a verbal take a look at. In it you will ask the capability problem to overlook about approximately some element for a term (it shouldn't be more than a couple of minutes). For example, you may ask your hassle to forget approximately the letter P. Tell them to faux that the letter P in no manner existed and to miss that you even knowledgeable them to overlook about it. Then ask them to recite the alphabet. People who are fairly or fairly suggestible will skip over the letter P (or a few factor letter you tell them to neglect about) and now not even recognize it. Once once more, if the man or woman you tried this check on skips over the letter you informed them to neglect, they'll be a great issue to area in on.

The Locked Hand Technique

The locked hand technique (additionally called the hand clasp technique) is every other bodily check that the trouble will must be willing to participate in. Like the light/heavy hand method, it's going to take a look at in reality how deeply someone can address the phrases you're pronouncing to them and what you are telling them to expect. Ask your problem to clap their arms together and maintain them collectively, palm to palm. Then inform them to interlace their hands. Make first rate that you keep constant eye-contact with them in the course of this take a look at and inform them to push their palms collectively as tightly as they may. Tell them to expect their fingers merging into one piece of stable flesh and bone. After a minute or , tell them to save you pushing and strive pulling their hands aside. Again, a capability manipulation undertaking will find it difficult to tug their fingers a long way from each different.

Chapter 11: Your Life Can Look Different

Is the life you stay the only you'll have decided on for your self? Most people inside the global may also solution negatively, but a few can be so bold as to reply with a powerful "Yes!" There is a school of notion that believes in the arrival of your private destiny. When the lives of many a success people are analyzed almost approximately how their fulfillment passed off, a few clues and styles emerge that element to achievement being a lot less approximately hazard and extra a made from how the thoughts capabilities.

What in case your success changed into genuinely depending on how your questioning styles were channeled to the manner you achieved your lifestyles? That could endorse that everyone need to gain way greater than they currently agree with viable, actually through manner of reprogramming the idea patterns of the mind. Can the mind be the critical thing to unlocking your success and paving the way to greatness?

The workings of the mind stay one of the least understood and least studied sciences in human history. In the 21st century, it's far turning into the location wherein extra medical project is being centered. As a natural organ, the thoughts is a complicated network of neurological pathways, specialised for loads of skills that outline our humanity. Harnessing mind functionality is largely the defining function of success-crammed residing.

Whether it's miles an addiction that you can't unfastened your self from or a rut you discover your self living in, no matter the stumbling block on your success is, it maximum probable stems from a incorrect way of thinking. The right data is that, that wondering sample can be modified with the aid of a few essential abilities and expertise of methods your brain can be reprogrammed for success.

Does it sound too suitable to be proper? Well take a look at on a touch earlier than you discard the concept as bunk. You also can find out a few contemporary wondering abilties that might transform your life.

NEURO-LINGUISTIC PROGRAMMING- A Rationale for Achieving Great Success

Neuro-Linguistic Programming (NLP) is a well-documented evaluation of the functioning of the human mind, applied to converting the outcomes of your lifestyles. Whether you locate your self looking for to transport as a great deal as the following level of fulfillment, or your lifestyles has actually spun out of control, there is some issue surely really worth inspecting within the tenets of NLP.

For most of the preceding millennium, human beings believed that fulfillment changed into a made from being born on the proper time, being given the right possibilities, and probable a hint luck. While fulfillment does have a few link to hard art work, most human beings by no means equate a success human beings as having "concept" their way to the top.

NLP gives a intent of "questioning" that demonstrates the capability of the mind to be re-calibrated and programmed to reap what earlier than everything seems simplest no longer feasible. Nelson Mandela once stated; "It's simplest impossible till it's far achieved." Most humans pay attention that very otherwise. They pay attention "It's handiest no longer possible until a person else does it." Inspiration, at the same time as it can encourage, does no longer always spur others without delay to trade and come to be a success. The mind desires to be modified in its thinking if we're to be those to do the not possible.

Even inside the twenty first century, the thoughts remains one of the most unexplored territories in human knowledge. Science stays "within the darkish" so to talk when it comes to understanding the workings of the thoughts. Over a hundred years of psychology have however now not satisfied mankind of the amazing strength of the thoughts.

With NLP, there has come a full-size range of strategies and abilties that make an effect on the functioning of the mind and mind. These techniques are available a number of understanding degrees, a number of which can be very number one to accumulate and execute, at the same time as others will take a excessive level of mastery to begin to put into effect.

Since NLP works on the thoughts's capability to count on and alter a person's truth via converting their method to reading and thinking about the situations they discover themselves in, NLP clearly has the capability to convert human beings. One of the goals of NLP is to make you into the sort of person who you'll need to live with within the world.

Think of a number of the people you may apprehend (both in my view or through media) that you reflect onconsideration on due to the fact the form of character you would love to be; perhaps due to their air of thriller, attraction, or have an impact on. Chances are that their fulfillment has a few roots in the strategies of NLP.

At the heart of the most a achievement human beings inside the worldwide, there's greater than simply difficult work, some correct fortune, and capabilities. There is a mind that thinks and perceives the area in a positive manner, and whether or not an character is aware about their wondering techniques or not, an lousy lot of what NLP is all approximately is a formalizing of the thinking abilities and conversational techniques humans have with each different that takes a number of us to outstanding successes.

The Basic Tenets of NLP

The critical definition of NLP is the use of techniques that re-application the thoughts on this sort of way as to enhance the existence of any character. Much of the concept of NLP has been collected from the observation of techniques and strategies utilized by a success people, which have been then documented and appropriated in the lives of others.

As the call NLP suggests, the techniques interest on the mind and senses (for this reason the term "neuro"). Secondly, the power of language, specially the manner we communicate to ourselves, entails a powerful catalyst for human behavioral exchange (therefore the time period "linguistic"). Language includes conversation, and with NLP, an improvement in self-verbal exchange and speaking with others ensuing in a sophisticated building of relationships with others or more a success wonderful thinking. And in the end, the term programming suggests that the thoughts may be reprogrammed to assume along a one-of-a-kind pathway.

So at the same time as some of the techniques used are properly-documented, the idea is that any approach that demonstrates an much less high-priced fulfillment fee at influencing our questioning, and therefore behavior, is a way that need to be hired as part of an

NLP technique to developing our very personal happiness and success.

Some techniques will encounter as obvious, and self-obvious. Others may furthermore appear modern, and best to be finished alongside side experts. Ideally, the severa degrees of the strategies will help individuals adjust bad conduct and damaging wondering styles ,and as such bring about an improvement in residing existence and finding fulfilment and success.

It is suggested that as one begins offevolved to discover the techniques utilized in NLP that one makes entire use of the diverse techniques noted, and appropriates those techniques that result in lasting exchange. As such, wonderful people want a few techniques over others. Many even forget about about using a few strategies as unscientific. The backside line should now not be to verify clinical veracity even though, however as an alternative to find out severa competencies and physical activities to enjoy their impact upon oneself due to the fact the man or woman.

NLP comes from the approach that no two human beings revel in existence in the same manner. Since we're everybody experiencing lifestyles from a unique, person enjoy, there may be no unbiased experience in lifestyles, however rather an basically sensory enjoy that for everybody is interpreted thru their non-public eyes. As such, it stays the person's lifestyles enjoy and potential to research, rationalize, and make experience of the experience that assists them in coping with life problems and navigate the path of their life in a way that brings about both their fulfillment or failure.

NLP attempts to assist the character to move an extended way from the failures, setbacks, and terrible wondering that holds them decrease returned and prevents them from moving beforehand, and instead include a sequence of capabilities that encourage, improves overall performance, and displays a a fulfillment lifestyles journey that benefits the person and those in their location. As such, NLP is a movement that has many people to the betterment of humanity. NLP clients attempt to upload and expand the range of skills and techniques that flow into humanity in advance into a hit careers, life styles, and choices for the overall development of humanity as an entire.

Chapter 12: What Is NLP used for?

NLP can be applied in a whole lot of situations. Essentially, the underlying principle of NLP is to look people be triumphant or conquer life troubles or setbacks. This can be as simple as converting a few pattern of thinking that leads to poor behavior, or breaking a horrific dependancy that results in negative consequences, or perhaps overcoming a phobia that has constrained one's capability for prolonged periods.

Further than certainly concerning the cognitive thoughts, NLP furthermore goes on to apply mind techniques that effect the conduct of others, and also can hire hypnosis as a manner of changing wondering and converting terrible or detrimental conduct.

NLP is beneficial in negating the patterns in a single's existence that bring about stagnation, cyclical, or recurring behavior, and mainly in assisting one set the course for achievement in existence. If you have were given the selection to carry out well and stay an outstanding lifestyles, NLP can take you there. Even with regards to enhancing your reminiscence, constructing better relationships, or inclusive of self perception for your existence, NLP offers quite various techniques and capabilities that will help you accumulate this.

Our Sensory Perception of the World

So there's a announcing in NLP circles that "The Map is Not The Territory." What this indicates is that on the equal time as you look at a map, you aren't seeing the general picture. You see a instance of the place and the area of critical objects, but you have not visible what the area looks as if or explored its fullness in any sense via any approach. If the map had been the territory, there is probably no want for us to tour, as we can also want to just have a check maps all day and revel in places for ourselves as they're. (Thank goodness that's not real, due to the fact I love journeying).

In the same way, existence isn't professional in all its fullness with the aid of manner of the use of our revel in of it. We enjoy so little of lifestyles on our very personal. The sum of all of the opinions is what makes lifestyles, however the fullness of what is possible with life is what we need to find out, and we need to accomplish that with the help of what lifestyles gives us to revel in. Most human beings will agree that existence gives us masses, however only a few mother and father get to revel in a life we actually need.

This is due to the truth we normally tend to check life through very tainted glasses (some rose-coloured, sure, but unluckily just a few). There is not masses that we can do approximately our enjoy of life to start with as we deliver all of our facts approximately life via, first our 5 senses. What we see, touch, flavor, experience, and perfume paperwork a massive a part of our enjoy of the world and the manner we enjoy it. Since maximum of these sensory critiques are associated with our mind through neural pathways, we get to shape a image of the arena we adore and dislike through those sensory stimuli.

Let's test an instance. As a child, you may find that your dad and mom mashed up your meals whilst you were little so you didn't need to bite it as hundreds. They may have fed you with a spoon in location of a fork, and while they had been feeding you, can also have sung songs to you making the whole, olfactory, auditory, and sensory experience a happy one. The reality which you enjoyed the feeding experience, and likely giggled and laughed in reaction, created many real emotions saved via your thoughts, and if the enjoy modified into a selected one which have end up repeated often, those feelings of happiness and pride must have formed sturdy signs of happiness in you.

Today as an adult, you could find which you despite the fact that like eating soft food with a spoon and probable taking note of some music at the same time as you gain this, as this engenders in you a feel of happiness. So mainly if you are feeling rather down, nostalgic, or under the climate, the concept of this consolation-meals-state of affairs is a actual choose-me-up and takes you to a "happy vicinity." Not that there may be some thing wrong with this; all I'm trying to factor out is one truely contemporary, but simple, idea. Your mind is now programmed to enjoy this experience and discover consolation in it, really because of the reality, in the formation of the neural pathways, whilst you have been more youthful, it shaped outstanding emotions as regards to the event and notwithstanding the reality that recollects the ones emotions within the identical or similar state of affairs nowadays.

So how does this relate to NLP? Well, that's in reality the essential precept in operation. It is viable to application the thoughts in this type of way as to make you react both certainly or negatively. Let me give an reason behind...

So even as you had been taking element in your mashed up meals in a glad and comfortable environment, more youthful Paul emerge as moreover receiving his mashed up food via a spoon, but in a totally one-of-a-type surroundings. Not being hungry on a specific day, he changed into fighting the forced food away and developing a huge extensive range. At the equal time, his dad and mom were arguing with each wonderful and his mother changed into shouting at him, in frustration, to eat his meals. The auditory, olfactory, gustatory, and tremendous sensory perceptions began to be connected to a very terrible revel in and feelings of frustration, anger, worry, confusion, and probable more. All making up for a few very horrible establishments associated with the revel in of eating. Today, Paul does now not like gentle meals in any respect, nearly loathing the feel, and seldom eats in an environment with many people round, who opt to consume on my own.

Now those can be excessive examples, but they very properly illustrate the factor I want to depart with you. Sensory perceptions are sincerely that, they may be neutral, however the environments we have them in frequently dictate how we respond to them into the future. Of path, the complexity of human experience does not advise that we're simply programmable as human beings, a number of us change willfully (probable forcing ourselves to like mashed food, regardless of the reality that we had a horrible experience in advance than). But there is a lot to be said for this idea that we can be programmed in this way through sensory revel in, and it's far in our unguarded moments that that is maximum real. There are such a whole lot of areas in lifestyles in which this may be established to be the case.

Chapter 13: Installed Predetermination

More than all of the sensory perception installations in our thoughts, we are also a instead complicated blend of installations that surround our ideals-those topics we have been taught through others (circle of relatives and pals) and that we've got processed as being truth, having veracity, and being of the sort of nature to us that we must mold our lives considerably round them. Also, our research brought on through interplay with one of a kind humans, weave into a tapestry that shapes how we see others and ourselves and deal with them and ourselves subsequently.

This super clean out that builds into us typically gives us the impetus to direct our lives in either a fine or poor (typically a aggregate of each) manner. If left up to those pre-programmed installations, we have a tendency to move along through existence primarily based completely mostly on those and one among a type new ones that keep forming. Very regularly, even though, it is the equal vintage reinforcing conditions that we hold experiencing if we don't take the time to have one-of-a-kind testimonies in our lives. It works like this.

The application we run often leads us into new evaluations, much like the program we have just run and so this gadget is strengthened to run once more ,giving us each exclusive similar revel in. Let me illustrate by way of the usage of using a private story related to my daughter. She is currently six-years-vintage ,and my goal for her existence is to provide her a glad kids and permit her enjoy the sector as lots as she will be capable of, as rapid as she can be able to address it.

So what takes area is that from time to time we've a exceptional experience. That would possibly range from going to the concern park (honestly fun) to in reality being thrown up into the air and being stuck (moreover sincerely amusing). My daughter's preferred reaction to some thing on this "a laugh/class is to "do it once more, daddy." So we repeat the fun enjoy of throwing her up into the air, until she is bored with it (that during no way takes vicinity, so until I can not reap this any further).

Now at the equal time as she is in want of a few aspect a laugh to manifest that makes her feel actual, what do you watched she wants to do? Well she normally asks to visit the state of affairs park (which unfortunately we can not always do), or she asks to be thrown up into the air (which maximum of the time I can do). The reality that this extraordinary feeling of connection to her dad is being strengthened is high-quality for constructing relationships but the moderate negative is available in, in that she is restricting her revel in of fun sports activities and conditions through continuously asking for the identical component.

So at instances, I have to assist her to understand that she is probably capable of moreover have amusing if we go to the water-park, or take an afternoon enjoy to the zoo. At first, it come to be hard to persuade her, thinking about that her revel in of a laugh changed into on the issue park, no longer the water-park or zoo. But after the number one go to to every of these locations (which moreover grew to end up out to be amusing), she now gives a few choices of locations to move. But my goal is not to just fill her lifestyles with an entire lot of amusing reviews if you want to have a top notch choice of factors to do. The aim is to educate her that the number one experience she had of an area might have been fun and that if she in no way had the revel in, she could probably in no way apprehend if it changed into fun or no longer.

I truely have a quite tough time nonetheless convincing her that going to an area she has in no way been might be amusing. The attraction very frequently rests at the tried and tested truth that daddy could in all likelihood not take her to a place that she possibly wouldn't enjoy. So over again, she is drawing on antique reports of her dad, to alternate her programming to simply accept as actual with that new evaluations also can deliver the equal happy outcomes or may additionally moreover even exceed them. The life talent I preference she is being programmed with is to understand that life gives many stuff which have no longer been experienced in advance than, and that new research are a few factor to encompass and tackle so that you can bypass correctly through life and to make the most of it.

Recently, we had a unhappiness in that we went to the situation park however the large crowds at the day made us pull away. I knew that my daughter might get pissed off via status in prolonged strains, but all she may additionally want to peer grow to be that the day grow to be not going to be a laugh. I described to her that she can also no longer revel in the day, but to no avail. She changed into sulky and moody as we walked another time to the auto (a trait I hate in humans-due to a few horrible NLP in my very own existence).

Now I had a few options in how I ought to cope with the situation. I may want to react badly and display my disapproval and make the day even greater terrible. I also can need to get angry at the side of her, once more reinforcing horrific behavior. Instead I did the subsequent. I said to her that there had been different a laugh topics we ought to do. She didn't accept as true with me, and knowledgeable me that the first-rate component she preferred to do changed into visit the subject park in any other case we ought to surely pass lower decrease returned home. I contemplated it, however inside the again of my mind preferred to redeem the day and use it to illustrate a lesson and train her a existence-capabilities.

Now she is crazy approximately Oreos (who isn't?), and nowadays an Oreo café opened up at one of the branch shops. Unbeknown to her, that's in which we were headed. When we arrived, she modified into lots a great deal less moody, however now not in her popular glad place. As we walked into the café, I noticed a moderate smile on the nook of her mouth. After some splendid Oreo treats, I had a satisfied girl once more.

Perhaps some of you are pronouncing this is indulgent parenting, however wait permit's examine it a touch. What did I gather by using the usage of this technique? I changed the want for happiness (one every body have) with some element else that made her glad. (A extremely good new first time experience for her). So we effectively traversed the minefield of keeping our lifestyles in a superb place. Secondly, I gave her the revel in of some component else a laugh, despite the fact that she had the frustration of the previous revel in.

Did she get that, you may ask? Oh, maximum absolutely. We had a long communicate in some unspecified time in the future of the day (on and rancid) approximately how we're able to in spite of the reality that make the maximum of life even if we've got matters that disappoint us. We went right now to an excellent paintings exhibition (my six-365 days-vintage already suggests herself to be an art gourmand). We discovered Nathan Sawaya's ART OF THE BRICK. She changed into brief to detail out three representations of well-known paintings finished in Lego i.E., Mona Lisa, Starry Night thru van Gogh, and The Scream through manner of Edvard Munch. What a terrific enjoy, and so you can forestall off this story a quote from Nathan Sawaya – "Art makes higher human beings, art work is critical in information the sector and paintings makes human beings satisfied." Undeniably, art is not non-compulsory. I'd want to function –and nor is happiness.

All in all, I expect we did a higher venture of using NLP to find out about life, and with a piece of good fortune my daughter's destiny life reviews might be "tainted" via way of using this one. When subjects cross incorrect for her (and that they genuinely will at instances), she will be able to are searching out particular studies of lifestyles that satisfy her, now not be slowed down in distress by using the usage of manner of the disappointments so that you can come.

Oh, but some of the extra terrible thinking among you're already saying, "Yes but how will she ever discover ways to push via the matters that can deliver her great pleasure but earlier than the entirety may additionally moreover deliver sadness?" – one lesson at a time human beings, one lesson at a time. Besides, there may be NLP for that too, and are we able to want to train her the type of perseverance on the manner to achieve a few final cause, even though it's a protracted way fraught with trouble and disappointment along the manner? You wager.

Chapter 14: Program Update

So really, if we expect in a sure course and that thinking consequences in great behavior, and that conduct outcomes in fantastic results that we've on our global and on others, then it'd be proper to say that a alternate within the give up result we've got in our international and on others want to necessitate a exchange in our questioning. The filters we use to dictate our reactions to stimuli and responses from others may be altered, and if we do adjust them, we routinely engender trade in the results we enjoy.

This method that we have a long way more control at the consequences of our lives and the success we collect than what many humans assume. Many accept as proper with that fulfillment is concerned in fulfillment, loads more might also attribute it to who you understand, but few consider that fulfillment can be programmed inside the thinking about the character.

But while a chunk desirable fortune is useful, and who we apprehend without a doubt affects on our success, if chatting to successful humans extensive about the reasons for their success and what it took to get them there, the distilled version of the information they offer, much more likely elements to a pattern of wondering that nearly guarantees fulfillment.

This is what NLP attempts to discover in others and mirror in human beings for comparable outcomes. In the subsequent chapters of this e-book, we're capable of look at the strategies and techniques that we will rent to interrupt out of the mindsets and filters that limit our success in life, and notice how we're able to negotiate the trails life places in advance than us for a completely unique greater a fulfillment final consequences to our lives.

Clearly, this isn't always the very excellent element inside the global to do and inside the starting we anticipate, how is it possible to negate each clear out and update them with new ones. We can not cross lower back and relive our lifestyles in any conscious way a remarkable way to apprehend that we have got got changed our wondering.

The beauty of NLP is that, with some targeted wearing activities and potential tendencies, we are able to empower the mind to override conventional techniques and discover its functionality to be reprogrammed to the extent that we enjoy a change in consequences in regions we frequently within the beginning feel will in no way alternate.

I truly have effectively employed this reprogram method in the lives of the numerous college college students I train who hate school or arithmetic (my difficulty), and watched them go from concerned places or damaging apathy to fulfillment, regularly on the top of their grade with the aid of using now not plenty coaching them the idea and art work they need, but rather along all of the concept and art work, education them to help their mind reply absolutely to the artwork they may be studying. The effects are quite wonderful.

So NLP isn't continually even best for you as an individual. Your use of NLP may be made to steer others for the higher. You can affect the outcomes that others experience, in fact with the aid of the use of strategies that open up their thoughts to new possibilities, and with out them even being conscious that you are having a direct effect on them.

www.ingramcontent.com/pod-product-compliance
Lightning Source LLC
Chambersburg PA
CBHW071444080526
44587CB00014B/1992